ACTION RESEARCH FOR SCHOOL LEADERS

Dean T. Spaulding
College of Saint Rose

John Falco
College of Saint Rose

PEARSON

Boston Columbus Indianapolis New York San Francisco Upper Saddle River
Amsterdam Cape Town Dubai London Madrid Milan Munich Paris Montreal Toronto
Delhi Mexico City São Paulo Sydney Hong Kong Seoul Singapore Taipei Tokyo

Vice President and Editorial Director: Jeffery W. Johnston
Senior Acquisitions Editor: Meredith D. Fossel
Editorial Assistant: Andrea Hall
Vice President, Director of Marketing: Margaret Waples
Marketing Manager: Christopher Barry
Senior Managing Editor: Pamela D. Bennett
Project Manager: Kerry Rubadue
Production Manager: Susan Hannahs
Senior Art Director: Jayne Conte
Cover Designer: Karen Noferi
Cover Art: Fotolia
Full-Service Project Management: Sudip Sinha/Aptara®, Inc.
Composition: Aptara®, Inc.
Text and Cover Printer/Bindery: Courier Companies, Inc.
Text Font: Times Lt Std

Credits and acknowledgments borrowed from other sources and reproduced, with permission, in this textbook appear on the appropriate page within the text.

Every effort has been made to provide accurate and current Internet information in this book. However, the Internet and information posted on it are constantly changing, so it is inevitable that some of the Internet addresses listed in this textbook will change.

Copyright © 2013 by Pearson Education, Inc. All rights reserved. Printed in the United States of America. This publication is protected by Copyright and permission should be obtained from the publisher prior to any prohibited reproduction, storage in a retrieval system, or transmission in any form or by any means, electronic, mechanical, photocopying, recording, or likewise. To obtain permission(s) to use material from this work, please submit a written request to Pearson Education, Inc., Permissions Department, One Lake Street, Upper Saddle River, New Jersey 07458 or you may fax your request to 201-236-3290.

Library of Congress Cataloging-in-Publication Data

Spaulding, Dean T.
 Action research for school leaders/Dean T. Spaulding, John Falco.—1st ed.
   p. cm.
 Includes bibliographical references and index.
 ISBN-13: 978-0-13-138104-9
 ISBN-10: 0-13-138104-0
 1. Action research in education.   2. Educational leadership.   I. Falco, John.   II. Title.
LB1028.24.S73 2013
370.72—dc23

2011037439

10 9 8 7 6 5 4 3 2 1

PEARSON

ISBN 10:   0-13-138104-0
ISBN 13: 978-0-13-138104-9

CONTENTS

Preface   viii
About the Authors   xi

Chapter 1 THE ROLE OF SCHOOL LEADERS IN SCHOOL IMPROVEMENT—PAST, PRESENT, AND FUTURE   1
Past to Present   1
Leadership Matters   4
Bootstrap Data: Information That Helps   6
> *Summary   8   •   Key Concepts   9   •   Discussion/Reflection Questions   9   •   Activities   9*

Chapter 2 USING RESEARCH TO SOLVE THE PUZZLE OF SCHOOL IMPROVEMENT   10
School Administrators' Use of Research   11
Types of Research Administrators Encounter   14
Applied Research Versus Vendor-Based Research   15
> *Summary   17   •   Key Concepts   17   •   Discussion/Reflection Questions   17   •   Activities   18*

Chapter 3 ACTION RESEARCH AND THE INQUIRY PROCESS   19
What Is Level 1: Classroom-Level Action Research?   19
Action Research, Naturally   20
Steps in Level 1: Classroom-Level Action Research   21
> *Summary   26   •   Key Concepts   26   •   Discussion/Reflection Questions   27   •   Activities   27*

Chapter 4 SCHOOL-LEVEL ACTION RESEARCH   28
Steps in Conducting Level 2 School-Level Action Research   29
Identifying the School-Level Issue   31
Developing an Action Research Team   31
Types of Action Research Teams   33
> *Summary   35   •   Key Concepts   35   •   Discussion/Reflection Questions   35   •   Activities   36*

Chapter 5 ANALYZING DATA AS AN ACTION RESEARCH TEAM   37
How to Analyze Data as an Action Research Team   38
Three Main Data Points for Needs Assessment: An Overview   39
Analysis Techniques   41
> *Summary   44   •   Key Concepts   44   •   Discussion/Reflection Questions   44   •   Activities   45*

Chapter 6 EXAMINING PAST RESEARCH, AND REVIEWING AND CRITIQUING CAUSE–EFFECT EXPERIMENTAL RESEARCH 46

Examining Past Research and Literature 47

Databases 48

Selecting from the Review of Literature 49

Full Text and HTML 50

The Action Research Team and the Review of Literature 51

Analyzing the Review of Literature 51

Creating a Literature Matrix 52

How to Critique Cause–Effect Research 53

Experimental Research 54

How Should Action Research Teams Critique Experimental Research? 55

Causal–Comparative Research 57

Summary 58 • Key Concepts 59 • Discussion/Reflection Question 59 • Activities 59

Chapter 7 CRITIQUING AND APPLYING CORRELATIONAL AND SURVEY RESEARCH 60

Correlational Research 61

Caution About Drawing Causality 61

The Correlational Coefficient 62

Types of Correlational Research 62

Statistical Significance 63

Using Correlational Research 64

Critiquing Correlational Research 64

Survey Research 65

How to Critique Survey Research 66

Survey Design and Development 69

Adapting and Adopting Instruments from Survey Studies 69

Summary 69 • Key Concepts 70 • Discussion/Reflection Question 70 • Activity 70

Chapter 8 CRITIQUING AND APPLYING QUALITATIVE RESEARCH 71

Qualitative Research 71

Methods Used for Qualitative Research 72

Access to Subjects and Settings 72

Examples of Qualitative Research 74

    Types of Qualitative Research   74

    Using Qualitative Research   75

        Summary 75 • Key Concepts 76 • Discussion/Reflection Question 76 • Activity 76

Chapter 9 GATHERING DATA FROM STAFF AND OTHER STAKEHOLDERS   77

    Gathering Feedback with the Survey   78

    Why Feedback Is Needed   80

    Methods for Gathering Feedback   80

    The Survey and the School Administrator   80

    Effects of a Poorly Constructed Staff Survey   81

    Basic Components of a Survey   81

    Tips for Writing Quality Items   85

    Administering and Collecting the Survey   87

    Methods for Administering Surveys   87

        Summary 91 • Key Concepts 91 • Discussion/Reflection Questions 91 • Activity 91

Chapter 10 STEP 2: DEVELOPING A PROGRAM FOR SCHOOL IMPROVEMENT   92

    Developing Quality Programs and Initiatives   93

    Aligning Need to Program Activities   93

    Introduction of the Logic Models   94

    Why Use a Logic Model?   94

    Logic Model: Basic Building Blocks   95

    Showing Change with a Logic Model   99

    Using Logic Models   99

    Using the Logic Model with Your Action Research Team   100

        Summary 100 • Key Concepts 100 • Discussion/Reflection Questions 101 • Activity 101

Chapter 11 STEP 4: IMPLEMENTING THE PROGRAM OR INTERVENTION WITH FIDELITY   102

    What Is Fidelity in Action Research?   103

    Developing a Fidelity Checklist and Observational Protocol   104

    Evaluating Professional Development   106

    Evaluating the Fidelity of Professional Development   107

        Summary 108 • Key Concepts 109 • Discussion/Reflection Questions 109 • Activity 109

Chapter 12 STEP 5: GATHERING AND ANALYZING DATA 110
    Gathering and Analyzing Standardized Data 110
    Three Levels of Assessment Data 110
    Different Types of Standardized Measures 112
    How to Critique Standardized Measures 114
    Confusing Reliability and Validity 115
    Applying Different Types of Standardized Measures to Your Logic Model 115
        Summary 117 • Key Concepts 118 • Discussion/Reflection Question 118 • Activity 118

Chapter 13 STEP 6: REFLECTING AND MAKING MODIFICATIONS TO THE PLAN 119
    Reflecting on the Logic Model to Determine Success 120
    Reflecting on Activities 121
    Reflecting on Outputs 121
    Reflecting on Intermediate Outcomes 122
    Reflecting on End Outcomes 124
    The Action Research Team and Making Modifications 126
        Summary 126 • Key Concepts 127 • Discussion/Reflection Questions 127 • Activities 127

Chapter 14 CASE STUDY 1: ADDRESSING HIGH TEACHER TURNOVER AND LOW STUDENT PERFORMANCE 128
    Background and Personal Characteristics of a School Leader 128
    Step 1: Forming the Action Research Team 129
    Step 2: Conducting the Data Analysis 130
    Step 3: Conduct a Review of the Literature 132
    Your Turn . . . 132
    Step 4: Collection of Additional Data from Stakeholders 132
    Your Turn, Again . . . 132

Chapter 15 CASE STUDY 2: DECREASING THE PERFORMANCE GAP BETWEEN GENERAL EDUCATION AND SPECIAL EDUCATION POPULATIONS 133
    Background and Personal Characteristics of a School Leader 133
    Level of Preparedness 134
    Step 1: Forming the Action Research Team 135
    Step 2: Conducting the Data Analysis 135
    Your Turn . . . 136

Chapter 16 CASE STUDY 3: ADDRESSING BEHAVIORAL PROBLEMS AND LOW STUDENT PERFORMANCE   138
    Background and Personal Characteristics of a School Leader   138
    Level of Preparedness   139
    Step 1: Establishing an Action Research Team   140
    Step 2: Analyzing the School   140
    Your Turn . . .   142

Chapter 17 CASE STUDY 4: IMPROVING LOW ELA SCORES AT THE ELEMENTARY LEVEL   143
    School Leader   143
    School District   143
    Level of Preparedness   144
    Step 1: Establishing the Action Research Team   145
    Step 2: Analyzing School Data   145
    Your Turn . . .   147

References   148
Index   151

PREFACE

As authors, we recognize that our mission is not to retrain school leaders to become professional researchers; however, we do believe that the purpose of this book is to assist current and future school leaders in building the research skills necessary for improving schools by increasing student achievement. While some may disagree about what types of training school leaders for the 21st century will need to attain to be effective, one thing is clear: Without the ability to use and conduct research, school leaders will continue to stay on the same track that many have worked on for decades.

In addition to gaining knowledge and better understanding of research methods, we also believe that an underlying mission of this book is to help you, the school leader, to become a more effective leader as part of the research process itself. Anyone can collect data in a school building. The real challenge is getting one's teachers and staff onboard, motivated, and empowered as a result of participating in the research process. That is the real work and a focus of this book. We believe that an effective school leader is one who is constantly demonstrating to staff that research is a critical element for a school community, and therefore this book will focus on three main areas:

- To provide school leaders with the technical background and skills to read and *critique* current educational research
- To provide school leaders with methods in which they can *apply* current research and research methods for collecting and analyzing data in their buildings
- To provide the framework for school leaders to *conduct* their own building-level action research for ongoing building improvement

Chapter 1 focuses on the role of the school leader and summarizes how school administrators and leaders have worked to improve buildings and education in general: past, present, and future. In this chapter you will also learn about different leadership prospectives in the quest for building and school improvement, as well as a discussion about what a school leader is and the important roles school leaders play in school improvement.

Chapter 2 examines the skills that administrators and school leaders need in their efforts to improve schools. In this chapter you will learn about the lack of interest in or use of research by school officials and how there is an increased emphasis on the need for a research-based skills set for school administrators and leaders, particularly in conducting research in their own schools.

Chapter 3 discusses the different types or levels of action research, one of which is action research for the classroom teacher. In this chapter you will read about the role of action research in the classroom and its role in helping teachers research and differentiate effective from ineffective instruction.

Chapter 4 focuses on what is referred to in this book as building-level action research. Building-level action research is the focus of this book. This is where an action research team will develop and use a team approach: identify a problem or issue in the building that needs to be addressed through examining school data; examine past research about how best to address this problem; and work to implement, monitor, and research a building-level improvement plan.

Chapter 5 focuses much more in depth on how the action research team should go about examining and analyzing the school's current data in order to identify a gap that needs to be addressed.

This is followed up in Chapter 6, where you and the action research team learn how to incorporate past research into the analysis process. Chapter 6 focuses on critiquing cause–effect research, and how this type of research can be used by the action research team in developing its plan.

Chapter 7 focuses on examining and critiquing correlational and survey research. The chapter also presents possibilities about how the action research team can incorporate these two important types of research approaches into their analysis and ongoing work.

While the previous chapters have examined quantitative research, Chapter 8 focuses on elements of qualitative research and the important role this type can play in the action research team's efforts, as well as in school improvement. This chapter provides an overview of the main types of qualitative research. In this chapter you will also learn how to critique qualitative research.

In Chapter 9 you will learn about how you and your action research team can collect additional self-report data from teachers, staff, and other stakeholders in the school building through administering surveys and other related tools. These data are important for many reasons: determining what your staff thinks about an issue, understanding staff's view and issues, or gathering important feedback from staff about training and professional development in which they have participated.

Chapter 10 shows how you and your action research team can work collaboratively in developing a program or action research plan to address the issue that has been identified. This chapter provides guidance in how to incorporate into your program what you have learned from reviewing the literature or how to plan and build a logic model to guide your action research project.

Chapter 11 focuses on how to go about implementing your program or action research plan and how you and your team can go about ensuring that the program is being implemented with fidelity.

Chapter 12 focuses on how to gather both formative and summative data throughout the action research process. This chapter also highlights standardized measures, what constitutes a standardized measure, and how to critique these tools. In addition to using more about standardized measures, this chapter encourages you and your action research team to think outside of the box and include various types of standardized measures to create a more rigorous logic model for measuring and monitoring the success of your efforts.

Chapter 13 is an important chapter because it provides you and your action research team with a framework for using the logic model as a tool for reflection.

Chapters 14 through 17 are short case studies depicting the actions of building administrators and school leaders using the five-step action research process presented in this book.

ACKNOWLEDGMENTS

There are many people who helped make this book possible. I would like to thank my research assistant Courtney Wayman for her time, energy, and dedication, working on this project daily for the last 2 years. In addition, I am forever grateful to my team of internal editors: Jen Dilorio, Kristina Osborne-Oliver, and Meghan Morris. I could have not done this without you. I also want to thank Drs. Dianna Newman and Deborah Kundert for letting me bounce ideas off them and members of The Evaluation Consortium at the University at Albany/SUNY. In addition, I thank members of my department at The College of Saint Rose for once again enduring another colleague who is writing a book; and Evan Seiden, Z Score Inc., for his encouragement, support, and willingness to stop work at any time and listen to my latest idea for this book. Finally, I want to thank all my CITE students from Yonkers, Brooklyn, and Long Island for their help, assistance, and feedback as I piloted these materials and ideas over the last 15 years. Thank you all!

D. T. S.

Special thanks to Kathleen Roark for her assistance in helping to make this book possible. Thank you to the students, faculty, and administration at The College of Saint Rose. And thanks to Erika, for her never-ending patience and support.

J. F.

Both authors would like to thank the reviewers of this book, including Paula Cordeiro, San Diego University; William G. Cunningham, Old Dominion University; Michael DiPaola, College of William and Mary; Joyce Logan, University of Kentucky; Laura Summers, University of Colorado at Denver; Karen Tankersley, Arizona State University. Stephen F. Midlock, University of Saint Francis; Emily Pettersen, Rockwood School Districk; Joy Rose, Westerville City Schools; Misti Williams, University of North Carolina at Greensboro.

ABOUT THE AUTHORS

Dean T. Spaulding, Ph.D., is an associate professor in educational psychology at The College of Saint Rose in Albany, New York. He teaches educational research methods and program evaluation. He is one of the authors of *Methods in Educational Research: From Theory to Practice* (2010) and the author of *Program Evaluation in Practice: Core Concepts and Examples for Discussion and Analysis (2008)*. He has conducted program evaluation for the National Science Foundation (NSF), U.S. Department of Education, U.S. Department of Labor, New York City Department of Education, and New York State Department of Education, to name a few. His evaluation work includes instructional coaches and teacher professional development, E2T2 Technology Integration programs, online professional development (OPD), elementary school counseling programs, Teacher Leadership Quality Partnerships programs, reading and literacy programs, Math Science Partnerships (MSP), STEM, nanotechnology, changing teacher practices through action research, and Model Transitional Programs (MTP) for Students with Special Needs. For the past 15 years he has worked extensively with school-leaders-in-training in the greater New York City area. He continues to work with school data teams and school leaders to improve student performance. Dr. Spaulding also serves as a lead consultant with Z Score Inc. and can be contacted at DSpaulding@zscore.net.

John Falco, Ed.D., currently serves as Director/Faculty of The Institute for New Era Educational Leadership and Innovation at The College of Saint Rose in Albany, New York. In addition to offering course work for New York State School Building Leader certification, The Institute provides professional development opportunities to educators throughout upstate New York.

Dr. Falco has served as Superintendent and Deputy Superintendent in upstate New York, as well as Deputy Superintendent, Principal, and teacher in New York City.

During his career, Dr. Falco has led collaborations that secured over $40 million in federal and state grants. He has served as a principal investigator for a U.S. Department of Education Technology Innovation Challenge Grant and co-principal investigator for a National Science Foundation grant. He has partnered with C-Span and Time Warner on cable-in-the-classroom pilot projects.

Dr. Falco serves as co-editor of *K-12 Video-conferencing: Best Practices and Trends* (2007). He has contributed chapters to edited books and authored and co-authored research papers and articles in the area of technology. He has presented at conferences including the National Summit for Technology, Washington, D.C.; New York State Council of School Superintendents' conferences; New York State School Boards conferences; and New York State Reading Association conferences. Dr. Falco's work has been featured in *District Administrator* and *Education Week*, as well as PBS television and *Tech Valley Report*.

Dr. Falco has won several awards, including being honored by the New York State Computer and Technology Educators as Outstanding Superintendent for 2000–2001. In addition, he was honored as Outstanding Superintendent on the floor of the New York State Assembly and by resolution in the New York State Senate. Dr. Falco received the Malinda Myers Education Partnerships Award from the Schenectady NAACP in 2004. The New York City Council recognized Dr. Falco as Outstanding Citizen in 1992 and on January 6, 2006 was named in his honor by proclamation of the Mayor of Schenectady.

Dr. Falco received his B.A. from City College of New York; and M.S. from Long Island University; an M.Ed. from Teachers' College, Columbia University; and his Ed.D. from Seton Hall University.

CHAPTER 1

The Role of School Leaders in School Improvement— Past, Present, and Future

After reading this chapter you will be able to:

1. Understand significant events that have shaped the current educational environment.
2. Understand the importance of school leadership in a time of national and global economic transitions.
3. Understand the importance of school leadership in improving teaching and learning.
4. Understand the need for information (i.e., internal school-specific data) in improving teaching and learning.
5. Reflect on personal school leadership practice.

Vignette 1.1
Free Fall

Imagine, for a moment, that you as a school leader are Lois Lane or Jimmy Olsen. Imagine now that you have somehow been thrown from the top of a rather tall building. Imagine the sense of helplessness and feeling unprepared for what is about to come as you are hurtling toward the ground. Imagine now that there is no Superman. As a school leader you may experience feelings similar to Lois and Jimmy (i.e., free falling), but probably in far more realistic situations than our imagined vignette.

PAST TO PRESENT

Lois and Jimmy had a sense of helplessness and felt unprepared for what was to come as they fell through the air. As a school leader you may have had similar feelings but in very real, not imagined, situations. If you have, it may be because you have a clear understanding of the responsibilities, challenges, and opportunities of your role. No previous generation of school leaders has been mandated with having not most but every student learn and achieve at high levels. You are facing these challenges in a far more complex environment than in any previous age of schooling—today's stage has broadened to include the world.

The past several decades in education have marked a transition that mirrors the nation's economic needs. And like the future of the nation, and all transitional periods, it is marked with uncertainty.

Certainty was a hallmark of the Industrial Age model of education. Schools mirrored factories, and uniformity was valued. Like the factory plant, schools were divided into departments. Departments consisted of skilled specialists. Students, as though on an assembly line, moved from one specialist to another throughout the course of the day. Content knowledge was "poured" from the specialist into the "empty vessel" at each step along the "assembly line." Departments were headed by the most skilled specialists who, like foremen, would oversee the workers' productivity (Taylor, 1967).

Although schools, for the most part, retain the structure and vestiges of the Industrial Age, the education required for a new generation must far exceed that model. According to Darling-Hammond (2010), "At least 70% of U.S. jobs now require specialized knowledge and skills, as compared to only 5% at the dawn of the last century, when our current system of schooling was established" (p. 2). Today's students not only need skills that will allow them to compete, but they will likely have more jobs during their lifetime than previous generations. Even today's workers will have more than 10 jobs before they are age 40 compared to two or three jobs for many workers in the 20th century (Darling-Hammond). Despite the specifics of future job markets, we know that a quality education for every student is essential.

Significant events in education have brought us to the present. Historically, policy and decisions regarding K–12 public education have taken place at the local levels. As the United States transitioned from a predominantly agricultural nation to a predominantly manufacturing nation, schools transitioned as well. Schools prepared students for the emerging job market without federal policy or funding.

However, beginning in 1965 and during the ensuing decades, the federal government has played an increasingly larger role as education is viewed more and more as critical to economic competitiveness and as a vehicle for eliminating inequality of educational outcomes for its citizens.

In 1965, as part of President Lyndon Johnson's War on Poverty, Congress passed the Elementary and Secondary Education Act (ESEA). The Title I part of the law specifically provides funding to schools and school districts with high percentages of economically disadvantaged students. In part, the law recognized the disparity in the funding of education at the local level and attempted to compensate schools that were disadvantaged financially.

In 1983, President Ronald Reagan's National Commission on Excellence in Education produced a report, *A Nation at Risk,* which conveyed to the public that the nation's schools were failing. In very powerful language the report notes that "the educational foundations of our society are presently being eroded by a rising tide of mediocrity that threatens our very future . . . what was unimaginable a generation ago has begun to occur—others are matching and surpassing our educational attainments" (National Commission on Excellence in Education, 1983). The report was not without controversy or political implications but has set the educational agenda from its publication to the present. Since the release of this report, school improvement has been an important national issue.

The reports seemed to have had an impact on school reform efforts. Tyack and Cuban (1995) wrote:

> In the decade from 1983 to 1993 . . . reformers adopted various strategies to increase the academic achievement of students. When one approach to reform did not appear to work, innovators quickly turned to alternatives but generally left the original reform laws and layers of rules and regulations in place. As a result, exhortations for change and mandated practices often worked at cross purposes. . . . Confronted with contrary reform demands, practitioners sought refuge through strategies of accommodation, resistance, and hybridization. In the process, schools changed reforms as much as reforms changed schools. (p. 78)

However, a significant shift in federal policy did not take place until 6 years after the release of *A Nation at Risk*. From the passing of ESEA in 1965 until its 1989 reauthorization, evaluating school quality was based on inputs (e.g., per pupil funding, student–teacher ratios). Over the last 2 decades, outcomes (e.g., student achievement) have become an important measure of school effectiveness. This shift occurred as a result of the standards-based movement of the 1990s (Doran, 2003).

In 1989, President George H. W. Bush convened a meeting of the nation's governors at which certain priorities were identified:

- Ensure all children beginning school are "ready to learn"
- Increase high school graduation rate to 90%
- Demonstrate competency in English, math, foreign languages, science, civics and government, economics, arts, history, and geography in 4th, 8th, and 12th grade
- Provide students with a safe educational environment, free of drugs, alcohol, firearms, and violence
- Achieve top ranking in the world in math and science
- Attain a 100% literacy rate among adults along with ensuring that American workers have the skills that will enable them to "compete in the global economy." (McGuinn, 2006)

Following this summit, then-president Bush unsuccessfully attempted to have Congress pass legislation that would have called on the states to voluntarily establish academic standards linked to these goals. This legislation encountered resistance from people who thought the federal government should not interfere in education. Others were critical of the proposal to develop academic standards without additional funding for schools that served disadvantaged students.

During his tenure as governor of Arkansas, Bill Clinton had played an active role at the education summit, and as president of the United States he pursued the development of academic standards. In addition, education reform efforts in the 1990s not only focused on pushing for standards but also for the development of student assessments (Danielson, 2001). Some advocates for assessments argued in favor of student portfolios as a tool for accountability, but high-stakes standardized tests have become the norm (Wolf, LeMahieu, & Eresh, 1992).

As president, Clinton made some progress with the push for academic standards. Goals 2000 legislation provided states with federal funds to develop academic standards. The legislation incorporated many of the goals previously identified by President Bush but also incorporated National Standards for Arts Education. The 1994 reauthorization of ESEA, known as the Improving America's Schools Act, went further:

- States were required to develop standards in math and language arts in order to receive Title I funding.

- States were required to develop assessments that were aligned with these standards. These assessments were required to be administered to students once during the later elementary school years (sometime during Grades 3 through 5), once during the middle school years, and once during high school.
- States were required to identify schools that failed to meet these standards and to take corrective action.
- School choice funding for Title I students was introduced.

Goals 2000 set the stage for the subsequent **No Child Left Behind (NCLB) Act** with the principles of standards-based/outcome-based education, assessments aligned with standards, and corrective action for failing schools. In 2002, the NCLB legislation reauthorized and shifted the focus of ESEA (McGuinn, 2006). "No longer content to provide access to education for traditionally excluded student populations, we are now demanding that these students receive good quality educations," wrote Scott Abernathy in *No Child Left Behind and the Public Schools*. "In other words, we are demanding equality of quality" (2007, pp. 2–3).

NCLB legislation went even further than the federal legislation of the 1990s in requiring the development of academic standards, the administration of regular assessments linked to the standards, and measures to hold schools accountable to these standards. In addition to developing standards in math and language arts, NCLB called on the states to create standards in science. States were also required to assess students annually between third and eighth grade. In the early 1990s, initial conversations about standards included proposals for using portfolios as a tool for assessing student work (Wolf et al., 1992). By the time NCLB was introduced, the focus was strictly on standardized testing. NCLB also featured the following:

- States are required to demonstrate proficiency in these standards by 2013.
- States are required to issue report cards on schools. The data included on these report cards must show aggregate test score data as well as the outcomes of subgroups.
- Schools are required to show "adequate yearly progress" (AYP) among their students.
- Schools failing to make AYP 2 years in a row must be identified as "schools in need of improvement." If these schools receive Title I funds, they must devote 10% of this funding to professional development activities focused on improving student achievement. Any school considered a School in Need of Improvement (SINI) must also provide students with the option of transferring to other schools.
- All schools must hire "highly qualified teachers."

LEADERSHIP MATTERS

Vignette 1.2
The Mission

In the course of doing some consulting work for a very large American technology company, I had occasion to meet several prominent leaders of the organization. At one such meeting, I was asked about the school leadership preparation program at the college. The question was somewhat rhetorical: "Are you teaching them to be accountable?" Accountability, as well as productivity, he explained, were essential components of the private sector but seemed to have no bearing on public schools. In fact, compensation and continued employment were not based on accountability or productivity in public schools as they are in the private sector.

> "What would happen," I asked, "if a team leader or manager of your company spent 90% of his or her time on tasks not central to the mission of your organization?"
>
> The man laughed at the absurdity of the question and submitted that any individual not focused on the mission would not last long in his organization.

The sole purpose of schooling is student learning, and what you do each and every day as a school leader matters. What you do is far more powerful than what you say. Where you place your time, effort, and energy matters because it demonstrates what is valued and what is not valued in your school. You are a role model for anyone aspiring to be a school leader. Based on the priorities evidenced by your daily practice, what exactly would someone in your community be aspiring toward by modeling you?

As part of the process for admission to our School Leadership Certificate program, candidates are interviewed. Part of the interview process is intended to determine what the candidate is aspiring to be. The simple answer to the question is "school principal." But the response is far more complex. Every candidate has a perception of the principal's role based on his or her own experience. Principals do what aspiring principals see them do. If the principal's priorities are seen to be handling difficult situations with students, teachers, and parents; scheduling; budgeting; and meetings and paperwork, then that is the level to which the candidate will largely aspire. If the priorities are perceived to be helping teachers improve their practice, fostering collaboration to improve teacher practice, establishing an environment that supports inquiry and creativity, and fostering the use of meaningful data to inform instruction, then that will become a large part of the candidate's aspirations.

Invariably, candidates generally cite examples of school leaders' strengths that focus on managerial aspects of the principal's role. Although those managerial aspects are important, they are not the essence of the role. Heifitz (1998) speaks to both technical and adaptive change in *Leadership Without Easy Answers*. He notes that demonstrating mastery of technical change (i.e., managerial skills) builds credibility and capacity in moving an organization toward adaptive change. In essence the managerial tasks are necessary but not the primary purpose of the school leader's role. *The only things that are significant in any school are teaching and learning.* Everything else, no matter how important it may seem, exists to support teaching and learning. Any activity or individual in a school that does not recognize its support role risks becoming self-serving and counterproductive to the mission. It is what takes place in that classroom only that positively or negatively affects student learning and achievement.

However, the second most important factor that has an impact on learning and achievement is the school leader. Research done by Mid-Continent Research for Education and Learning (McREL) found a positive correlation between strong leadership by principals and student achievement (Marzano, Waters, & McNulty, 2005). The researchers identified 21 responsibilities of school leaders (e.g., communication, knowledge of curriculum, instruction, assessment, monitoring/evaluating, situation awareness) that have a positive impact on student achievement. Building on this research, Waters and Cameron (2007) noted that strong leadership by a principal might not be effective if the principal directs his or her efforts to matters that will not have an impact on student achievement. Waters and Cameron wrote, "There are many practices and activities on which a principal can focus the attention, energy, talent, and other assets of the school. Not all of them have the potential to positively influence student achievement. They may be important in the running of a school, but not essential for improving achievement" (p. 9).

BOOTSTRAP DATA: INFORMATION THAT HELPS

> **Vignette 1.3**
> **CSI**
> Recently, a colleague asked me if I was familiar with *CSI*. Yes, I was. No, he informed me, not the television program, but what he labeled *Curriculum Scene Investigation*. It is more an event than a series, he said. The day test scores are announced, and for several days thereafter, school leaders in districts across the country stand studiously over the fresh "curriculum corpse." Chalk lines outline the body. District ribbons barricade the scene, prohibiting too much public scrutiny. The investigation thoroughly examines every group and subgroup—and then some—that failed to achieve. Investigators must ponder both potential fixes as well as blame. The investigation concludes, the body is buried, and business goes on as usual, until next year's episode of *Curriculum Scene Investigation*. It's a clever analogy, not fully accurate, but accurate enough to give pause.

State assessments are designed to evaluate student achievement, not inform individual instructional practice. The annual assessment is a "snapshot" in time. The data may help school leaders in making decisions regarding curricula or programs. The data also inform the public of the school's academic standing (a reflection of the quality of your school), but many school leaders are not completely sure what to do with them.

Douglas B. Reeves (2008) reported the following based on three visits to schools across the United States:

- One overwhelmed principal had not even opened the previous April's testing data.
- Of 15 principals, 14 confessed to never having used the costly district data warehouse.
- One school leader printed "every test score, grade, and demographic characteristic of every student on chart paper" in preparation for meetings with teachers.

In his article, "The New Stupid," Frederick M. Hess (2008) noted:

> I fear that both "data-based decision-making" and "research-based practice" can stand in for critical thought, serve as dressed up rationales for the same old fads, or be used to justify incoherent proposals. Because few educators today are inclined to denounce data, there has been an unfortunate tendency to embrace glib new solutions rather than ask the simple question, "What exactly does it mean to use data or research to inform decisions?" (p. 12)

Hess (2008) posed an important question: "What exactly does it mean to use data or research to inform decisions?" But let's take it one step back to an essential question: What information do you need to make decisions regarding teaching and learning?

As a school leader you are the receiver of multiple transmitters regarding teaching and learning in your schools. You are the recipient of expansive testing data. You are the recipient of "research-based" programs, whether district mandated or self-selected. You are the recipient of "curricula" designed by textbook companies. Indeed, we could continue the list.

During the course of your career you have or will be the recipient of one or several new programs that are perceived to be the answer to the challenges of improving teaching and learning. Many may be good; however, the tendency in education has been to drop programs as "new" ideas come along. The cyclical nature of implementing–dropping–implementing in a sense obfuscates the real work of understanding individual classroom processes, such as student engagement and teaching strategies, if you let it.

> **Vignette 1.4**
> **Another New Program**
>
> The new and much heralded "Hold the Book Upside Down" program has been mandated by your district. It has been vetted through committee, publicly lauded by the superintendent as research based, and approved by the Board of Education. One half day of professional development is provided for all teachers. Fifteen percent of your faculty call in sick on the professional development day.
>
> There is no specific professional development for you as a school leader. Rather you are told to attend sessions with the teachers. The opening speaker is high powered, research based, and infectious in his enthusiasm. It's not just the reading material that's turned upside down; it's the individual as well. It is a program designed to go across the curriculum so teachers and students in every classroom will be standing on their heads. Charts and comprehensive data regarding blood flow theory, cognition, and higher order thinking skills are displayed on the large screen. In the true spirit of collegiality, you too want to stand on your head.
>
> Shortly after implementation, several teachers complain to you that it may not be sanitary to share headrests and that the district did not purchase enough headrests for every classroom to participate. Furthermore, they ask, "Why don't the physical education, music, and art teachers have to stand on their heads?"

On his blog on *Edutopia*, Stephen Hurley (2010) provides evidence of the cyclical nature of trends in education that he has seen come and go during his 25 years of teaching. He refers to these trends as "the bandwagon principle" and writes, "My bandwagon collection included books on mastery learning, portfolio assessment, cooperative classroom structures, technology integration, backward design, multimedia projects, personal learning paths, authentic task development, and, most recently, differentiated instruction and integrated curriculum."

All trends may not be created equally. For example, Schmoker (2010), in an article entitled "When Pedagogic Fads Trump Priorities," writes about the work of "solid research" to support differentiated instruction (DI). Schmoker describes some teachers as "frustrated" and notes that it "dumbed down instruction" and "corrupted effective instruction." Schmoker states, "As Byran Goodwin of Mid-Continent Research for Education and Learning, or McREL, has written, there is 'no empirical research' whatsoever for schools to adopt DI" (p. 22).

The bandwagon principle is not new. In a *New York Times* article entitled "Our Many Educational Fads and Fancies," George Trumbull Ladd of Yale University states that "School teachers are always experimenting but do not seem to be getting anywhere." He concludes, in part:

> We have lost out of sight—or at least we have too little regarded—the end of education in our ceaseless and largely futile experimenting with the nonessentials of the means. Our great need is an improved personnel among our teachers, and thus an enlarged personal freedom for them in their difficult and too often thankless task. (p. SM 13)

Professor Ladd's article was published on June 18, 1916. In essence Professor Ladd is saying we need quality teachers who are given the freedom to teach. Some 80 years later, Diane Ravitch (2000), in her study of school reform in America, powerfully reiterates the same sentiment:

> If there is a lesson to be learned … it is that anything in education that is labeled a "movement" should be avoided like the plague. What American education really needs most is not more nostrums and enthusiasms but more attention to fundamental, time-tested truths. It is a fundamental truth that children need well-educated teachers who are eclectic in their methods and willing to use different strategies depending on what works best for which children. (p. 453)

As a school leader you are the receiver for multiple transmitters. Many transmissions are mandated and require your compliance. However, the school has, under your leadership, control over internal processes. By *internal processes* we mean what takes place in the classroom. Regardless of the latest program, how do you focus on the improvement of instruction? And what information do you need to make decisions about teaching and learning?

Knowing what we may not yet know requires a fundamental belief that the purpose of school is teaching and learning and that any other purpose is self-serving. Therefore, the most significant activity in any school takes place in the classroom. The better informed we are about that activity within individual classrooms and across classrooms through practical research, the better we can advance student learning.

Vignette 1.5
Digging Deeper

During a post-observation conference with a high school teacher, the supervisor noted that class participation was very limited. The teacher said it was difficult for students who couldn't read to understand or participate in his course. Subsequently, the supervisor looked up the reading scores for the science teacher's class and learned that every student was at or above reading grade level. This information raised the level of the next conversation between the supervisor and the teacher.

The teacher and the supervisor might discuss any number of strategies that could improve student participation. More time spent on science-specific vocabulary or more hands-on activities might be among those discussed. However, the important concept here is that the impediment to the teacher's willingness to try new strategies was eliminated through practical information.

In a sense the science teacher had an "Aha!" moment. Glickman, Gordon, and Ross-Gordon (2007) cite McZirow's research as follows:

> Transformative learning refers to the process by which we transform our taken-for-granted frames of reference (meaning perspectives, habits of mind, mind-sets) . . . so that they may generate beliefs and opinions that will prove more true or justified to guide action. (p. 54)

Glickman et al. (2007) further cite Kegan who "contrasts transformative learning (changes in how we know) with informative learning (changes in what we know)" (p. 55).

There is no Superman. There are external forces, be they policy, testing, curriculum, or programs that may regulate or mandate you. However, there are no external forces that will "rescue" you.

Bootstrap data are defined as internal action research that provide information about teaching and learning in your school. Bootstrap data are not a program or a product. They constitute a process through which you can help yourself to improve teaching and learning.

Summary

Over time the focus of education has shifted from inputs to outcomes. Federal policy, once nonexistent in education, now plays a prominent role. Schools, like the larger global society, are in a period of transition.

Education reform often takes shape in "new" and "innovative" programs that may blur the mission of schooling. The single most important activities in any school are teaching and learning. School leaders are an essential part of improving student achievement.

The focus of school leaders must shift to internal processes. School-specific data for teachers and students can inform practice and improve learning outcomes.

Key Concepts

bootstrap data
No Child Left Behind (NCLB) Act

Discussion/Reflection Questions

1. As a school leader, what percentage of your time is spent daily on improving teaching and learning?

2. How do you currently use data to inform decisions about teacher practice and student outcomes?

Activities

1. Interview a retired or near-retirement teacher regarding the "trends" or various programs experienced over the span of his or her career. Ascertain what he or she thinks worked, what did not work, and why.

2. Discuss with colleague(s) the percentage of time spent daily in improving teaching and learning in their school. Also discuss how data are used to inform decisions about teacher practice and student outcomes.

CHAPTER 2

Using Research to Solve the Puzzle of School Improvement

After reading this chapter you should be able to:

1. Understand school leaders past use of research in making curricular and other decisions for school-level improvement.
2. Understand the similarities and differences between applied and vendor research.
3. Understand what action research is in general, and the different levels of impact action research can focus on to improve practice at the classroom, school, and systems levels.

Vignette 2.1
Trying New Strategies

I start every educational research class with a puzzle. The puzzle contains nine pieces. Next, I ask my educational leadership students how difficult they think the puzzle will be to solve. Their response: "Not very—after all, it's only nine pieces." But what I don't tell them is that the chances of solving the puzzle are about 3 million to 1. The secret to solving the puzzle is that you have to abandon the old strategies you normally use to solve a puzzle and try new ones. (But I don't tell them that.) Instead, I break the class into small groups and give them 20 minutes. The only other thing that I ask is for someone in the group to keep track of the strategies the team uses. Then I stand back, start the clock, and observe as the groups eagerly engage in trying to solve their puzzles. Twenty minutes passes, and no group has been successful. Enthusiasm levels are low, and frustration levels are high.

When I ask the groups to reflect on their strategies, the conversation usually goes something like this: One student will say, "I normally try to make a frame using all the straight-edge pieces first—but that strategy didn't work here because all the pieces have straight edges . . . so I didn't know what to do." Another student will say something like "I usually solve puzzles by trying to match the print or color. For example, if I am putting together a mountain scene, I will look for a puzzle piece that has snow and evergreens on it. With this puzzle, these strategies didn't work because the same picture is repeated across all the nine puzzle pieces. But I kept trying, hoping that they would eventually work. But they didn't."

I go around the room and other students tell me about the failed strategies that they tried. Then I ask the students why they didn't try other strategies when they realized that the ones they were using didn't work. Students usually respond that they would like to have tried other methods but didn't have any others to draw on. And so they kept repeating what they already know to no avail.—D.T.S.

When analyzing the puzzle activity, one theme begins to emerge: People do not necessarily abandon old strategies, even when it is clear that these strategies are no longer effective. As an instructor, it is fun to create dilemmas and watch students engage in the learning process; however, for many school leaders across the United States, such dilemmas are not an appropriate exercise for a research course or a professional development workshop. Yet for many school leaders (and their staff) trying to improve a low-performing or failing school without the necessary expertise is a frustrating and unfortunate reality (Beecher & Sweeny, 2008; Bernhardt, 2003; Chan-Remka, 2007).

Experts in leadership agree that if you, the new school leader of the 21st century, are to play a more prominent role in creating change in your school, you are going to need a new set of strategies or skills. Understanding research and critiquing research are at the top of the list of the proficiencies that have been linked with school improvement (Marzano, Pickering, & Pollock, 2001). In addition, studies have shown that for school leaders to improve schools, they must be able not only to understand research but also to apply research and research-based initiatives and interventions to their schools, programs, and classrooms (Marzano et al., 2001).

Although most school leaders have already taken an educational research course, basic introductory knowledge of educational research methods is not enough to assist school leaders in successfully addressing the complex issues they face today (Fusarelli, 2008). To be truly effective, Fusarelli and others suggest, today's school leaders need to acquire more advanced knowledge in critiquing current educational research studies, applying aspects of research to their schools, and conducting their own school-level and classroom-level action research projects with staff for ongoing improvement (Berry, Trantham, & Wade, 2008; Ellingsen, 2007; Ferguson, 2008).

SCHOOL ADMINISTRATORS' USE OF RESEARCH

There is a body of research in the leadership literature, albeit small, that examines how and why school leaders use research to improve their schools and increase student achievement (Bernhardt, 2005, 2009; Del Favero, 2009; Fusarelli, 2008). This area of research focuses primarily on answering research questions such as the following:

- What do school leaders think about research and its role in school improvement?
- How do school leaders go about using current research to inform practice and support curricular and programmatic decisions?
- What are the benefits and challenges to school leaders understanding and applying more research-based practices for ongoing school improvement efforts?

Research in this area is vital since it is important to know why school leaders use (or don't use) research to help guide their daily practice. Having a more in-depth understanding of school leaders' practices as they relate to research will assist those in educational leadership programs to develop better connections for school-leaders-in-training to engage and use the current research (Bernhardt, 2004; Fleischman, 2006; Gold, 2005). Such knowledge also would be beneficial for educational researchers thinking about how they can conduct their research in ways that will provide better "linkages" between the direct implications of their studies for improving schools and the classrooms of tomorrow.

Before you read any further and learn exactly what researchers in this area have found, take a moment and answer the questions in Self-Study Survey 1. Please answer each item as honestly and as accurately as possible.

> **EXHIBIT 2.1** **Self-Study Survey 1: School Administrators' Use of Research**
>
> Directions: Read each item and respond accordingly using the scale provided.
>
> **1 = Strongly Disagree 2 = Disagree 3 = Slightly Disagree**
> **4 = Slightly Agree 5 = Agree 6 = Strongly Agree**
>
> | Items | SD | | | | | SA |
> |---|---|---|---|---|---|---|
> | 1. I often find research confusing. | 1 | 2 | 3 | 4 | 5 | 6 |
> | 2. I find research studies are often contradictory and never come to a solid conclusion. | 1 | 2 | 3 | 4 | 5 | 6 |
> | 3. I think most research studies have an agenda. | 1 | 2 | 3 | 4 | 5 | 6 |
> | 4. Overall, I believe research is important. | 1 | 2 | 3 | 4 | 5 | 6 |
> | 5. To be an effective school leader one must have a strong technical command of educational research and research methods. | 1 | 2 | 3 | 4 | 5 | 6 |
> | 6. Research studies often focus on variables that have little relevance for real day-to-day issues in schools or classrooms. | 1 | 2 | 3 | 4 | 5 | 6 |
> | 7. If one research study says one thing, I can easily find another that says the exact opposite. | 1 | 2 | 3 | 4 | 5 | 6 |
> | 8. When reading research I often do not know what to believe. | 1 | 2 | 3 | 4 | 5 | 6 |
> | 9. As a school leader, it is important that I show my staff that I have a strong command of educational research. | 1 | 2 | 3 | 4 | 5 | 6 |
> | 10. Schools could do a better job if research would just let us do what we know. | 1 | 2 | 3 | 4 | 5 | 6 |

Research on how school administrators use and apply current research suggests, overall, that school administrators do little in the way to consult studies in guiding their practice, selecting curriculum, or identifying proven practices for improving classroom instruction (Fusarelli, 2008). Although many professionals in the field recognize the clear importance of understanding and using research to drive school improvement efforts, the use of research has not been a practice that has been widely "embraced" by the school leader community (Streifer & Schumann, 2005). Fleishman (2006) and others note that there are many reasons why school administrators may be apprehensive to use research as part of their professional practice. According to Fusarelli and Fleishman, here are some reasons why:

1. *Lack of consensus among research studies.* Have you ever read a study and wondered, will this be the answer to our school's problem, only to realize at the end of the study that its findings were inconclusive? If so, don't worry: You are not alone. One of the reasons noted by Fleishman (2006) and Fusarelli (2008) why school leaders have gradually moved away from using research is because they feel that research studies typically do little to reach a consensus or solid conclusion. One study will say one thing; another study

will say exactly the opposite. In the end, administrators feel that the results are vague more often than not, providing little assistance to them in making curricular or instructional decisions. According to Fusarelli, this perception about research plays a key role in why many administrators are saying "No thanks" to research and "Hello" to their gut feelings or personal opinions in how or why things should be done. (If you answered Agree or Strongly Agree to items 1, 2, or 7 in Self-Study Survey 1, you too hold the same perceptions and see research as something that is difficult to pin down, often contradictory and confusing.)

2. *Variables having little relevance to the classroom or school.* Administrators also noted that many times researchers are interested in studying or isolating variables that are not the variables educators are interested in (Ferguson, 2008; Fusarelli, 2008). In many cases, research studies will examine the relationship between educational variables or test a hypothesis that has little or no relevance to the classroom or the day-to-day challenges faced by many teachers. Although some school leaders can see the important contributions research studies make to extend and support our general knowledge on topics or issues, too many leaders have come to their own conclusions about research and its usefulness (Johnston & Lawrence, 2004). (If you answered Agree or Strongly Agree to items 4, 6, and 10 in Self-Study Survey 1, you too tend to have perceptions that lend themselves to seeing research as something that has little relevance. You see research as having little implication in solving the "real" issues or problems that plague classrooms and schools on a day-to-day basis.)

3. *Having a hidden agenda to their purpose.* Some school leaders are suspicious of research—and for good reason. As noted by Fusarelli (2008), some school administrators do not see research as an unbiased source of knowledge, but a process that often comes with many conditions attached. For example, Fusarelli notes that in some instances research-based programs on state department of education adoption-approval lists have been shown to be developed by companies with personal ties to key state employees. (If you answered Agree or Strongly Agree to items 3 or 8 in Self-Study Survey 1, you too tend to hold perceptions that research is something used by those who have a hidden agenda and that research should not be trusted.)

4. *Lack of technical background in research methods.* Perhaps one of the biggest barriers to school leaders using research to make decisions is that many school leaders lack the technical background to critically analyze, interpret, and apply findings from the research studies they read (Fusarelli, 2008; Marzano, 2003). Many school leaders read what appears to be a quality study but are left wondering "Is this a rigorous study or not?" at its conclusion. Despite the fact that school leaders have taken courses in research and research methods at both the undergraduate and graduate level, in most cases this coursework focused heavily on "traditional" research methods. In addition, coursework in many research classes focus on hypotheses-driven research, experimental designs, and randomization of samples and other research-related techniques. Overall, these courses have not focused on the practical application and utilization of research in a field-based setting such as a school, where many ethical and infrastructural constraints need to be considered. Although working knowledge of technical research methods is certainly important, previous coursework in educational research most likely stopped short of providing an understanding of the application of research and research methods in a school or how a school leader should go about conducting a research study in a school (Calhoun, 2002; Glanz, 1999). (If you answered Agree or Strongly Agree to items 5 or 9 in Self-Study Survey 1, you believe that research

is something over which those in a leadership position should have a strong command. You believe a leader uses research to provide a vision for the school community, and a leader serves as an example to staff and others about the importance of research.)

TYPES OF RESEARCH ADMINISTRATORS ENCOUNTER

One reason many school leaders may be skeptical of research is the type of research they are confronted with daily. School administrators interface with two main types of research: applied research and vendor-based research.

APPLIED RESEARCH. Applied research is conducted by professional researchers who are from institutes of higher education (Lodico, Spaulding, & Voegtle, 2010). The purpose of applied research is to expand our general understanding and knowledge about an issue or phenomenon. In addition, applied research makes implications or recommendations for practice. In educational research, these implications can include anything from specific changes in classroom instruction to changes in school infrastructure (e.g., how things are organized). As described, many administrators feel that applied research does not address the specific problems they face in trying to improve their schools. For example, an applied research study could examine the relationship between parent involvement and the academic achievement of students. The study concludes that student achievement is greater when an adult who is present in the home also interfaces with the school. Although findings from this study certainly expand our knowledge and understanding of the role of adult involvement in students' education, it doesn't necessarily shed light on how to increase parent or adult involvement in a school community where such involvement levels are low.

Applied research is typically disseminated through journals. Administrators reading applied research should be aware that not all journals are created equal. Journals have different submission policies and criteria for publication. After conducting their research studies, researchers usually write up their studies following a standard format used by the research industry. Educational research follows **American Psychological Association style (APA style)**. When they have completed their manuscript, researchers submit their work to journals; however, not all studies are automatically published. Some journals have a more rigorous review process than others. The journals with the most stringent process are peer-reviewed journals. Manuscripts submitted to **peer-reviewed journals** are critically examined by a team of the author's peers for content as well as the research methods and data. These studies are reviewed blindly, meaning the reviewers themselves do not know who the author is or the institution or agency. Studies reviewed by outside peers are returned to the journal's editorial board with one of three recommendations: publish, revise, or reject. Because of this extensive review process, studies published in peer-reviewed journals are considered to be of high quality. This doesn't mean that school administrators should leave it up to the experts to tell them a study is high quality. It does, however, provide school administrators with a "safety net" of some sorts, reassuring them, even if they don't understand all the technical aspects of the study's analysis, that the study is indeed rigorous and appropriate for the type of research being conducted.

Although we have focused this discussion so far on peer-reviewed journals, it is important to realize that school leaders also should pay attention to other journals that are not peer-reviewed. Scholarly journals also publish high-quality research studies and reviews of literature on a wide range of topics. These journals also utilize an editorial board or panels composed of professionals who critically review all the work considered for publication.

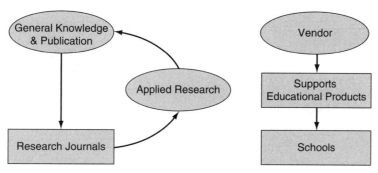

FIGURE 2.1 Applied Research vs. Vendor-Based Research

It also is important for school leaders to recognize that some journals focus on leadership theory, policy issues, and procedures in education. When researching an issue or topic, it is recommended that school leaders conduct a review of the literature from both areas: (a) journals that subscribe to sound research methods and (b) journals from the leadership area that focus on school change and improvement from a theoretical and practical perspective.

VENDOR RESEARCH. As discussed, applied research is published primarily in scholarly and peer-reviewed journals. School leaders have the choice to access this information or not; however, school leaders also are exposed to another type of research on a daily basis. **Vendor research** is conducted by for-profit companies (e.g., publishing houses) to support various curricula and programs purchased and used by schools. It is important for school administrators to recognize that the research supporting these products is for the most part not peer reviewed and, in most cases, has not been published or widely critiqued by scholars and professionals in the field. This research is often referred to as in-house research, whereby publishers hire researchers as consultants to work on these projects outside or to head up departments of research and evaluation inside their companies and organizations.

The purpose of vendor research is to conduct studies on products during their development phase to show that these new products are more effective than other educational products currently on the market. Keep in mind this is not to say that this research is not rigorous and that it should not be trusted; however, administrators need to be informed consumers of research when selecting curricula and educational products, and they must carefully examine the research methods that support the claims made for these products. Research and experts in leadership and school improvement note that selecting high-quality curricula and educational products that provide optimal learning experiences for students is one of the key practices associated with highly effective administrators (Marzano, Walters, & McNulty, 2005). Therefore, understanding research and critiquing studies to determine their quality are vital skills that new (and even experienced) school leaders need to foster and improve on (see Figure 2.1).

APPLIED RESEARCH VERSUS VENDOR-BASED RESEARCH

ACTION RESEARCH: WHAT IS IT? It is unfortunate that many school leaders feel this way about applied research and the importance of research in the quest for ongoing school improvement. Although remediating some of this distrust may go beyond the scope of this book, it is the purpose of this book to introduce school leaders to action research as a method for conducting their own research to help improve their own schools and students' futures.

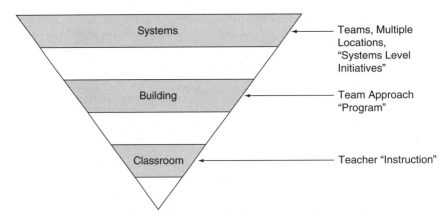

FIGURE 2.2 Three Levels of Impact

Traditionally, the focus of **action research** has been on teachers; research is conducted by teachers in their classrooms for the purposes of improving their practice and increasing student achievement (Berry, Trantham, & Wade, 2008; Hahs-Vaughn & Yanowitz, 2009; McLeod, 2005; Wayman, 2005). Although we applaud action research at the classroom level and believe it to be a powerful tool to help teachers recognize weaknesses in their instruction and make their instruction as optimal as possible, we see a disconnect in the literature on action research in that it often does not include school administrators. This we find ironic, since school administrators have been historically looked on as the instructional leaders for a school. We see action research as a vehicle for school administrators to foster relationships with staff members and the school community as a result of engaging the school community in the research process itself.

LEVELS OF IMPACT MODEL. In recognition of the potential power action research has for school leaders, we devised the **Levels of Impact model** based on the work of Corey (1953) and Stiggins and Duke (2008). The purpose of this model is to highlight the fact that certain types of action research projects have different purposes as well as different impacts or changes on the school culture. We have divided this model into three distinct areas: classroom, school, and system or district levels.

In **Level 1: classroom-level action research**, the teacher is the principal investigator or lead researcher. The focus and the overall purpose of this research is to determine what instructional practices are more effective in the classroom, and for the individual teacher to take action—modifying his or her pedagogy (Mertler, 2009).

Level 2: school-level action research accepts all the aspects of Level 1 but makes it a more collaborative effort, where the school administrator and staff select the variable or strategy that they want to research together. In many cases this school-level action research is spearheaded by a team. Although there are many names for these teams, they are often referred to as data teams, inquiry teams, or action research teams. Depending on the purpose and scope of the action research project, these teams are made up of the school principal, teachers, other staff, parents, community members, and even students. In most cases, school-level action research examines schoolwide data for a gap in student performance or behavior data where an improvement could be made. Typically, the course or plan of action in school-level action research projects is to implement a schoolwide program to address the issue. Continued data collection is conducted, and the program is monitored and refined along the way until the desired results are achieved (Mertler, 2009).

Level 3 action research is focused on district or systems-level change. **Level 3: system- or district-wide action research** is also a coordinated effort, but instead of focusing on a program being implemented in one school, Level 3 tends to examine the impact of larger initiatives. These initiatives tend to focus on the implementation of an educational program such as an after-school program, zero tolerance program, or a new curriculum initiative that spans the entire district, region, or state. In some cases, the interest in these action research studies goes beyond the immediate school leader and extends to the superintendent, the school board, and even the community at large (Mertler, 2009).

Summary

Casting aside old ineffective practices and taking on new ones is a challenging endeavor for even the most seasoned administrator. Experts in school improvement note that school administrators need to understand, more than ever, how to critique, apply, and conduct their own research. The research on how administrators use research to inform their decision making reveals that school leaders do not use current research to the degree that they should. Experts point to the lack of technical training in research methodologies, the disconnect between what variables researchers are examining and realistic issues occurring in the classroom, and the inability of many studies to reach solid conclusions as to reasons why many administrators look elsewhere when making curricular decisions.

School administrators should play an active role in reading both peer-reviewed research from scholarly journals. They also should know the ins and outs of research supporting the products and curricula they purchase and implement to improve student learning in the classrooms.

Aside from knowing the technical aspects of research and how to critique and apply research for school improvement, many administrators may have heard of action research. Some school leaders may have had the opportunity to participate in some action research of their own. In this book, action research is used in school settings to improve the professional practice of individual teachers in the classroom and in larger-scale efforts to create learning communities. Depending on the focus or purpose, an action research study may have different levels of impact in the classroom, school, or district. Effective school leaders should find a way to participate and to engage with staff to foster relationships and with the school community for any research project taking place at any of the three levels.

Key Concepts

action research
American Psychological Association style (APA Style)
applied research
Level 1: classroom-level action research
Level 2: school-level action research
Level 3: system- or district-wide action research
Levels of Impact model
peer-reviewed journals
vendor research

Discussion/Reflection Questions

1. Review the reasons why school leaders do not automatically think of consulting research. Have you ever thought this way? Why or why not?
2. School leaders noted several main reasons why they are reluctant to use research in their professional practice. One reason was that research studies often failed to investigate those issues shared by administrators and their instructional staff. If you were a researcher, what would you research in your school or district? Do you think that this would be of interest to other school administrators in other districts? Why or why not?

Activities

1. Re-create the puzzle activity described in the beginning of this chapter. Find some unusual puzzles and present them to small groups of administrators. Make sure each group is instructed to keep track of the different types of strategies they use when trying to solve the puzzle. Afterward, have the groups present the list of strategies each used and evaluate their effectiveness in helping them reach their final goal. Then have members of the groups talk about how this translates to practices and strategies they currently use in trying to improve their schools. Have these strategies proved to be successful? Why or why not?

2. Have each member of the class participate in Self-Study 1. Afterward, tally the results of the class to determine where class members are in regard to their use and perceptions about research. Use the data to drive the classroom. On what areas does the class of future school leaders need to focus?

CHAPTER 3

Action Research and the Inquiry Process

After reading this chapter, you should be able to:

1. Have a working definition of classroom action research.
2. Understand some general approaches to teachers conducting action research in their classrooms.
3. Understand research designs that do not lend themselves to classroom action research.
4. Know the basic steps for classroom action research.

WHAT IS LEVEL 1: CLASSROOM-LEVEL ACTION RESEARCH?

As described in Chapter 2, Level 1 action research is conducted by teachers individually in their classrooms (Bennett, 1994; Calhoun, 1994; Kelsay, 1991). Unlike Level 2, which examines school-level initiatives, Level 1 provides teachers with a greater degree of autonomy as they research for themselves what works for their students (Calhoun, 2002; Lodico, Spaulding, & Voegtle, 2010; May, 1993; Miller & Pine, 1990).

As you are probably starting to recognize, action research can take many forms. If you were to conduct a review of the literature on action research, you would quickly discover that one can take many different approaches. Although some action research approaches are bound to traditional research methods, others tend to move away from the more technical aspects of research and allow teachers to explore collecting data and improving their practices using much more informal methods.

The Level 1 research studies in this book are focused on action research that is intended to investigate instruction in the classroom. The purpose of these action research studies is to improve teacher instruction while at the same time improving student achievement and outcomes. These action research projects are tied closely to instructional methods and strategies, driven by student learning.

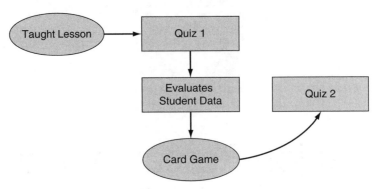

FIGURE 3.1 Natural Action Research

ACTION RESEARCH, NATURALLY

Although the main purpose of this book is to provide you, the school leader, with a framework for conducting school-level action research projects (Level 2), it also is important to recognize action research projects already could be naturally occurring in your school. In fact, it is our belief that action research naturally occurs in the classrooms of highly effective and reflective teachers (Bernhardt, 2004; Reilly, 2007). For example, consider the flowchart in Figure 3.1, in which a sixth-grade math teacher is teaching a lesson.

Let's say the teacher was teaching a lesson on multiplying positive and negative numbers. (Keep in mind, this could take place in any content area or grade level). The instructor teaches the lesson using what we will refer to as the "rule" method (e.g., a negative times a negative equals . . .), giving the students the rule they need to solve the problems and even modeling how to use the rule on the board. Following the instruction, the teacher assesses students by giving them a short quiz. After class, the teacher grades the quiz. The students' quiz grades are presented in Box 3.1.

Next, the teacher critically examines the quiz data and determines that, out of the 20 students, only a few have successfully demonstrated that they have mastered the concept. Finding this unacceptable, the teacher consults a journal for teaching mathematics in middle school and comes across a strategy for teaching multiplication of positive and negative numbers using a deck of cards. This alternative approach sounds interesting, and from previous experience the teacher knows that the students enjoy games. The next day, the teacher divides the class into

BOX 3.1	Student's Scores (Out of 100)		
Student 1	45	Student 7	24
Student 2	89	Student 8	77
Student 3	33	Student 9	89
Student 4	23	Student 10	19
Student 5	20	. . . and so on for the 20 students in the class	
Student 6	40		

small groups of three or four students and provides them with the following instructions: Black cards represent positive numbers, and red cards represent negative numbers; students have to keep track of their score as they play and trade their cards.

After playing the card game for a class period, students are given a second quiz. Afterward, the teacher compares student scores on quiz 1 to scores on quiz 2 and is encouraged by the results; all but two students have a passing score on quiz 2. Seeing the results, the teacher automatically integrates the card game into her teaching repertoire. From now on when teaching this lesson, she will use the alternative method whenever students appear to be having difficulty grasping the concept. Based on the data that she has collected and analyzed, the teacher has changed her practice.

As a school administrator, you would probably like all your teachers to be like this math teacher. But the big question is, is this action research? At its simplest form, we believe that it is. Here the teacher has used data to identify a problem in her classroom with students grasping the mathematics concept. She implemented a new variable, gathered data, analyzed the data, developed findings, and reflected and internalized the reflection to improve herself as a professional. In other words, she has taken another step in becoming a more highly effective math teacher in the classroom. In fact, the argument could be made that action research in its naturalistic form is what highly effective teachers do to improve their pedagogy and optimize their students' learning experience.

When taking a closer look at the steps described here, you might think that they sound a lot like good teaching. We could not agree more, making action research not only something that is expected of teachers but is required. In Level 1 research, the individual teacher is the one who determines what will be the treatment and how the impact in the classroom will be measured.

STEPS IN LEVEL 1: CLASSROOM-LEVEL ACTION RESEARCH

As discussed in Chapter 2, distinct steps are conducted for action research. This next section will walk you through the steps involved and place those steps within a classroom setting. In Figure 3.2, these steps are presented in a circle. Using a cyclical format conveys the underlying idea that action

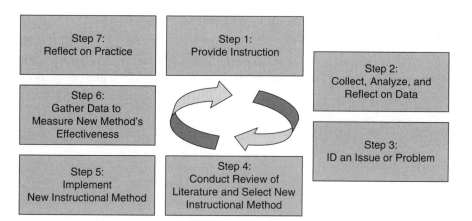

FIGURE 3.2 Steps in Classroom Action Research

research is ongoing. It is not something that a teacher would simply engage in once and then check off a list. In fact, effective teachers are continually engaging in action research, moving from one issue in the classroom to the next throughout the school year.

Step 1: Teacher Provides Instruction

In this step the teacher provides instruction to the class. Instruction is presented in the manner or method the teacher typically uses when teaching this lesson, skill, or concept. In the example in Figure 3.1, the teacher delivered the method of instruction through reciting a "rule" for the students to learn and then replicate with their own work. From the data gathered by the teacher (Box 3.1) you can see that the rule was not instantly "absorbed" by every student in the class.

Step 2 and Step 3: Teacher Analyzes Classroom Data and Identifies a Problem or Issue That Needs to Be Addressed

The first step in action research is to identify a problem or issue that needs to be addressed (May, 1993). Such a problem is usually identified through the teacher analyzing data that were collected through the use of a classroom-based or teacher-developed assessment. These assessments might include a quiz, a chapter test or unit test, or a student project or portfolio that the teacher administers to the class to check their learning of a new concept or skill. At its most informal level, a choral response or the teacher asking a question and students raising their hands also could be considered data on which a teacher could base a decision. All of these are common methods that a teacher might use to assess students as they engage in the learning process. Presented in Box 3.2 are the possible formal and informal measures teachers often use (Stiggins & Duke, 2008).

Next, the teacher needs to review the data collected by the in-class assessment of the students to determine if the students' performance in the classroom was acceptable. Take a moment to review the student scores in Box 3.1. If you were the teacher, would you find these results acceptable? If you answered "Yes," revisit the student data again. If you answered "No," that such performance was unacceptable, that is excellent!—a problem or issue in the classroom has been clearly identified, and this will be the problem that the Level 1 action research project will address.

Step 4: Teacher Conducts a Review of Literature and Selects a New Instructional Method

After recognizing a problem, the teacher sets out to find another instructional method (the potential solution) to put in place (Strickland, 1989). In research language, this "new" instructional

---

BOX 3.2 Possible Formal and Informal Measures

Ticket out the door	Chapter tests
Quiz	Unit test
Homework	Curriculum-based measures (CBM)
Student project	District benchmarks

strategy that the teacher will be using is the independent variable. It also is important to notice that, in this example, the teacher did not blame the students for their poor performance on the quiz or simply reteach the lesson the exact same way. We have worked extensively with educators on this process and have found ineffective teachers blame the lack of learning in the classroom on students: They weren't paying attention, they weren't interested, they aren't motivated—the list goes on and on. We also have seen ineffective teachers address the issue not by searching for a more effective or alternative method of delivery but by teaching the class again, repeating the same ineffective method. Sometimes, they may move students to the front of the room or utilize other methods that do not fix the root of the problem: the ineffective method of delivery.

For this type of action research, the teacher can go to a number of places to find strategies to implement when reteaching the lesson. One source for this example is journals on teaching mathematics. As discussed in Chapter 2, these journals could be research journals where such strategies have been "tested" in previous research studies and have evidence supporting their use in the classroom. While examining the literature, a teacher also might examine teaching journals in which the school district or school has a subscription. In reality, the teacher, in the preceding example, found the card game strategy in a journal that she subscribes to on teaching mathematics at the middle school level. Other sources of information could be colleagues who are teaching the same classes, instructional coaches, professional development personnel, and faculty from institutions of higher education.

Step 5 and Step 6: Teacher Implements New Instructional Method and Gathers Data to Measure New Method's Effectiveness

As you can see from Figure 3.3, the teacher collects observational data while students are playing the card game in their small group settings. In addition to the pre–post quiz data that are being collected, the teacher also walks about the room and collects qualitative data using an observational protocol. Although it is not uncommon for a teacher to walk around the room "monitoring" small group instruction, in this case, the teacher is also paying close attention to what students are saying as they engage in this activity. In fact, the teacher is using the observational **protocol** and writing down observations of student interactions as well as exact quotes of what students are saying and thinking as they work together. To get a

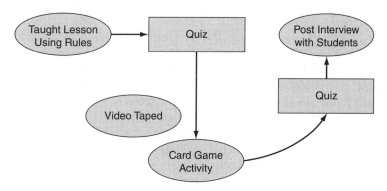

FIGURE 3.3 Example of Mixed Methods Classroom Action Research

> **BOX 3.3 Excerpt of Student Conversations Playing Math Card Game**
>
> STUDENT A: I think it is fun that we are playing a game in math class.
> STUDENT B: Me, too. Your turn.
> STUDENT A: Math is so boring. I didn't understand the stuff on the quiz, but I am getting it now.
> [Student A plays a card on the table and receives seven points.]
> STUDENT B: I know what you mean. If I could take the quiz again, I think it would go really good. Your turn.
> [Student B plays his card but makes a mistake in his calculation.]
> STUDENT C: You played a red three. It's red, so that makes it a negative three. And you played the red three on another red three. So that's two negative three's.
> STUDENT B: So minus six . . . a minus three minus another three.
> STUDENT D: It's not minus, it's negative. It's kind of like when your mother says you cannot go to the mall. That's a couple of negatives. Which if you think about it, means you can go to the mall, right?
> STUDENT B: I get it, so it's not minus but a negative. Two negatives make it a positive.
> STUDENT C: That's right. Just like when adults say things that they don't really mean.
> STUDENT A: Assume!
> STUDENT B: I totally get it now.

better idea as to the flavor of those conversations, an excerpt of the conversation is presented in Box 3.3.

You will also notice that the teacher has decided to video tape one of the groups as it worked through a card game exercise. In this case the teacher wants to collect what students are saying as they work on the game with one another. In this case, the teacher would analyze the video tape data later and use the findings to back up and support the work. In addition, the teacher also has notes she has taken while moving around the room, observing and listening to each of the groups.

At the end of the study, the teacher gathered additional qualitative data through the use of small focus groups with students. A **focus group** is a design used by many qualitative researchers to gather in-depth perceptions. Instead of conducting single one-to-one interviews, a small group of individuals is assembled. In a focus group, usually one commentator delivers the questions and focus group members respond individually. It is important when using a focus group approach to set the ground rules: Be respectful to each other and allow individuals to speak without interrupting. Here the teacher developed a set of open-ended responses in a tool that is called an interview protocol. The protocol helps to standardize the delivery of the open-ended questions so that the teacher action-researcher asks each of the questions exactly how he or she had envisioned. Presented below in Exhibit 3.1 is a copy of the protocol.

In addition to the observational and student focus group data, the teacher also administers another version of the quiz after students have engaged in the card game exercise for most of the class period. Following the quiz, the teacher analyzes student performance on the second quiz. Presented in Box 3.4 are the students' scores from the second quiz following their participation in the card game. Take a moment and examine the results. Now, compare this data to student performance on the first quiz. Is there improvement? Is this improvement now acceptable?

> **EXHIBIT 3.1** **Interview Protocol for Student Focus Group**
>
> This protocol was used by the teacher in the action research study to gather in-depth information or data from students. In a small focus group setting, the teacher asked students the following questions. The teacher took notes and audio taped the students' responses to obtain detailed information. The following are the open-ended questions the teacher used. Review the items carefully and see if there are any others that you would add to this protocol.
>
> How would you describe what positive and negative numbers are to another student?
>
> What do you think about the card game we used in class yesterday to learn about positive and negative numbers?
>
> Did the card game help you understand positive and negative numbers better? If so, explain how?
>
> What, if anything, didn't you like about the card game, or what made it difficult to understand positive and negative numbers?
>
> Would you recommend the card game to next year's class. If yes, how could it be improved to help next year's class understand positive and negative numbers even more?

Step 7: Teacher Reflects on the Findings

Like you, the teacher in this example is pleased with the increase in student performance. However, because of the one-group design, it is impossible for the teacher to be certain that it was the card game exercise that is responsible for the change in student performance on the second assessment. Revisit the design for this study presented in Figure 3.3. With a critical eye, can you come up with another possible explanation, other than the card game strategy, that may account for the observed increase in student performance on the second quiz?

In fact, if you take a few minutes to think about it, you can probably come up with a list of possible "alternative" explanations, right? Someone could conceivably argue that it was not so much the card game that made students improve but, rather, the fact that the class spent an extra period on something that the teacher might usually only spend one period covering.

Afterward, the teacher analyzed the video by playing it back. While watching the video, the teacher paid particular attention to the students: What were they saying? How were they

> **BOX 3.4** Post Data from Students (Out of 100)
>
> | | | | |
> |---|---|---|---|
> | Student 1 | 100 | Student 7 | 99 |
> | Student 2 | 90 | Student 8 | 100 |
> | Student 3 | 91 | Student 9 | 89 |
> | Student 4 | 89 | Student 10 | 79 |
> | Student 5 | 70 | . . . and so on for the 20 students in the class | |
> | Student 6 | 80 | | |

relating to one another? And how were they learning? For this action research study, there are two quantitative data tests (the pre- and post-quiz data) and three qualitative sets (e.g., video, observations, and focus group interview data). This type of approach would be considered **mixed methods,** combining methods in a single study so one avoids collecting just one set of data and collects both quantitative and qualitative methods.

Overall, a mixed methods action research study is a "richer" study but also helps address issues regarding the study's validity. For example, if the teacher in this example had only the pre–post data for student performance on the quiz, one could argue that the fact that the teacher spent an extra class period (e.g., more time) on the content, and if in fact the teacher had repeated the rule method again, the same type of results could also have been achieved. Although this is highly unlikely from a research perspective, one would not be able to successfully argue against this point.

Ultimately, one of the outcomes of having teachers engage in action research is so that teachers will "see for themselves" how effective certain instructional practices are for their students (in comparison to other not-so-effective practices) and hopefully, will adopt those new practices into their instruction. One of the reasons action research is so closely linked to discussions on changing teacher practices is that having someone engage in the process and see for themselves how effective something is greatly increases the chances of that individual changing his or her practices (Bennett, 1994). Having teaching staff continually engage in action research to "test out" different instructional strategies and classroom teaching methods not only can increase the quality of your teaching staff in the long run but also can greatly increase the performance of your student body (Calhoun, 1994; Sagor, 1992). In future chapters you will see that being an administrator or school leader who supports action research in your school will have a much greater impact on optimizing effective instruction in your school than will the individual who merely presents published research studies from a journal to his or her teachers at the latest staff meeting. What kind of leader do you want to be?

Summary

Action research can take many forms. Although the focus of this book is conducting school-level action research through the use of an action research team, it is important for school administrators and leaders to have a solid understanding of how action research has traditionally been used by teachers to improve their own practice. When applying action research in a classroom setting, a teacher would first identify an issue that needs to be addressed. These issues tend to and should focus on optimizing classroom time and instruction. Next, the teacher sets up the framework for the study and begins to implement new strategies to address the issue at hand. The teacher also sets up a method and timeline for collecting data. Once the data have been successfully collected, the teacher analyzes the data, reviews the results, and reflects on the overall process to determine whether or not to incorporate this new strategy into his or her teaching toolbox. All of this, of course, is based on the results of the teacher's action research study.

Key Concepts

focus group   mixed methods   protocol

Discussion/Reflection Questions

1. The purpose of classroom action research is to improve teachers' instructional practices and help teachers become more effective in the classroom. Being part of the process is one of the key ingredients to changing practices through action research. Reexamine Figure 3.2. What parts of this process do you think are most critical to helping teachers reflect and improve their instruction? What components do you think teachers should, but might not necessarily, use in the classroom?
2. What are some key areas in your school related to instruction that you would want your teachers and staff to investigate through action research? Create a list and be ready to share with the class.

Activities

1. Although action research is very useful, it also can be met with challenges. Examine the action research process in Figure 3.2, then generate a list of challenges that your teaching staff might face with these various steps. Think about how you would help further support your staff in meeting these challenges and carrying out the action research projects. Write a one- to two-page summary of what you would do.
2. Select a published action research study that interests you. Although you may find one published in a journal, you also might find action research studies published on the Internet. Review the study and apply the steps identified in Figure 3.2 to it. Are all these steps clearly delineated in the study? Have certain steps been overlooked? Critique the study and write a one- or two-page evaluation of the action research study. Be sure to note areas where you think the study could be improved.

CHAPTER 4

School-Level Action Research

After reading this chapter, you should be able to:

1. Describe in depth what Level 2 action research is and how it plays into school-level improvement.
2. Describe in detail the six steps that the school leader and action research team will need to take when following the action research process.
3. Explain the purpose of the action research team, its role and responsibilities, and your role as a school leader on that team.
4. Describe the purpose of the action research team and its different designs.

Vignette 4.1
Identifying "Real" Need

In October, Principal James Tyler attended a workshop on action research held by the district. Returning to his elementary school, he decided to have his staff engage in schoolwide action research. Although he is interested in improving student performance, he also secretly hopes that the project will catch the attention of the district superintendent. He hopes that success with the action research project will ultimately separate him from the other nontenured elementary principals in the district and put him on a certain path for tenure.

The following week, Principal Tyler observed fifth-grade classes during science instruction. He was unimpressed with the instruction the students were receiving. The teachers told him that they were doing inquiry-based science; however, there was little room for the students to work. Each of the five groups was spread around the room, huddled over a desk trying to conduct experiments. To Principal Tyler, the lesson looked messy and disorganized. In addition, Principal Tyler also was dismayed by the fact that at the end of the lesson, during the question and answer session, some of the groups had come to wrong conclusions. Based on his observations, Principal Tyler decided that his action research project would focus on a new science initiative in the school.

In the weeks to come, Principal Tyler selected a science program suggested by one of the vendors who frequented the building. The program was inquiry based, with learning objectives linked to the state standards as well as national learning standards in science. In addition, the program had an emphasis on "creating scientists" and focused efforts on making students feel that they were doing *real* science. As part of this initiative, the work stations in the classroom were designed to resemble science lab countertops. Students also were given lab coats (similar to the ones real scientists use) and designated locker space in their classrooms for the coats to be stored.

Instead of sharing the issue and what should be done about it with his staff, Principal Tyler decided to announce the idea at a school meeting, telling staff his concerns about the science instruction he had observed and about the student-centered program that they would soon be adopting. Professional development also was provided. Teachers spent an afternoon with a consultant learning about how they could make their lessons more "student centered" and thus provide students with motivation and interest to *do* science.

Overall, teachers were uncomfortable with the initiative and, more important, not certain as to its purpose. This discontent could be seen in teachers' interest during the professional development session. Teachers could be heard whispering from the back row, "Could someone tell me what was wrong with the old way?" and "What was wrong with the way we have always been teaching science?"

Later, once the initiative was underway, Principal Tyler observed classrooms and was pleased to see students wearing their white lab coats and engaged in student-centered instruction on their new lab countertops. The superintendent stopped by to see the program and congratulated Principal Tyler. The superintendent could easily see students being real scientists and engaging in *real* science, and he told Principal Tyler that he would be interested in seeing this year's science scores for students in the program.

At the end of the school year, the students took the state's standardized science assessment. When the results came back, Principal Tyler was eager to see the scores. He was overjoyed to report to his staff that the science program was a success. Ninety-five percent of the students had met or exceeded the state standards in science! His high spirits did not last long, however. From the crowd, one of the teachers announced that for the last 3 years, 98% of the students had passed the science exam district wide. So, in fact, the school had not improved but actually had declined a little in science performance.

Embarrassed, Principal Tyler went back to his office to think about where he had gone wrong. For months afterward, staff continued to talk about all the focus on science achievement when science achievement was not even the issue that needed to be addressed. Many staff members were upset that they had wasted so much time and energy on this when improving the school's English language arts (ELA) scores was needed much more. Only 46% of students in the school had passed the state's ELA annual assessment. Many of the teachers began to lose respect for Principal Tyler, his ability to lead, and his vision for the future.

STEPS IN CONDUCTING LEVEL 2 SCHOOL-LEVEL ACTION RESEARCH

As shown in the preceding vignette, school leaders who take on conducting *all* aspects of a school-level action research project will most likely become exhausted, as well as alienate themselves from teaching and school staff. Although the overall process used for Level 1 classroom action research is similar, school-level action research contains an initial step in the beginning that clearly separates it from all other types. Figure 4.1 illustrates the five basic steps, as well as an overview of each of the following steps.

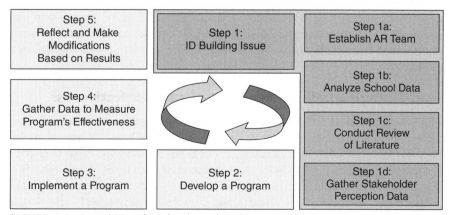

FIGURE 4.1 Steps in Level 2 School-Level Action Research

Step One: Identifying the Issue to be Addressed

In many cases, coming up with a list of issues that need to be addressed in a school or district is not something that most school administrators or leaders have trouble developing. In fact, it is probably quite the opposite. The bigger challenge is narrowing that list down to two or three issues that an action research team can focus on for school improvement purposes (Streifer & Schumann, 2005).

Within this first step are several substeps or activities that have to take place. First, the school leader should establish an action research team. This team would serve as the main research group throughout the action research process. The duties of the **Level 2 school-level action research team** would include, but are certainly not limited to, analyzing school data, conducting a review of literature and past research, and gathering additional stakeholder (e.g., staff) perception data.

Step Two: Develop a Program

After all the data groups have been carefully analyzed, the next step conducted by the action research team is to take all of the data, and what has been learned, and select or create a plan of action. Because of the level of impact that most school-level initiatives require, typically a program or some sort of intervention is selected to address the issue. In some cases, the action research team may decide that the best way to address the issue is to "take" aspects or components from evidence-based practices from previous research and combine them into a "customized" program to meet all levels of need in their schools. In addition to developing the program or initiative, at this point the action research team begins to frame out how it is going to measure the program's success. (An in-depth discussion is presented in Chapter 12 about measuring the effectiveness of your school-level initiative.)

Step Three: Implementation of the Program

After the action research team has agreed to *how* the issue will be addressed, the program (or treatment) is put into place. This is often referred to as program implementation. In most cases, at a school level, this type of approach requires training of teachers and/or staff about the new initiative and the new ways in which things will be done if the school is to see a different set of outcomes in the future. In addition, it requires that the various activities of the program or initiative be correctly executed by all the teachers or staff or whomever is responsible for delivering those activities (Bernhardt, 1999). Making sure that the program and its corresponding activities are done correctly is referred to by researchers as fidelity. In this step, the action research team will learn how to ensure that the program or intervention that it puts in place is being implemented with fidelity as well as how to collect formative data to monitor the program's progress.

Step Four: Gathering Data to Measure Program's Effectiveness

Determining whether a program or initiative was successful at addressing an issue or problem is something that every school administrator or leader dreams about being able to do. Although this may be the main focus for many in leadership, getting to this point (as you begin to realize) takes a lot of steps, planning, and hard work. In this step, determining what types of data must be collected throughout the entire process is discussed. Here the school leader and action research team learn about formative and summative data, research and evaluation matrices, and logic modeling—all designed to help keep the process on track as well as determine whether the practice was effective.

Step Five: Reflect and Make Modifications Based on Results

Although this is the last step in the school-level action research process, it is without a doubt one of the most important. In this step, the school leader and action research team learn how to critically examine the data from the program, reflect on the entire process, and use that to modify programs for the next cycle of programming. It is anticipated that in the next cycle of programming even more significant results will occur and the issue or problem that was selected initially will have been successfully addressed. This will allow the school leader and action research team to move to the next set of issues and begin work again, following the same action research process.

IDENTIFYING THE SCHOOL-LEVEL ISSUE

Today, the idea of using a team approach at the district, school, department, or classroom level to address an issue is quite common (Seaton, Emmett, Welsh, & Petrossian, 2008). Walk into any school, and you are sure to see small groups or teams of educators working diligently on a wide variety of topics or educational issues, from aligning curriculum to planning lessons to selecting the next literacy series for the school. One common way schools have used teams is in the analysis of annual high-stakes testing data (Del Favero, 2009; Streifer & Schumann 2005; Technology Alliance, 2005). As noted previously, schools have no shortage of data, and teams of teachers are often assembled in late summer or the beginning of the school year to peruse summative data. Although this work is important, many experts believe it comes too late to truly be effective for changing practice and improving student performance (Stiggins & Duke, 2008). Unfortunately, much of the data analysis process stops there and never matriculates into any real action or intention that can be studied in addressing the problem or issue.

Although there is no magical formula for determining the most effective composition for an action research team, it is important to recognize that those individuals who make up the team should be selected purposefully. In other words, the team should be composed of individuals who have a unique set of skills and content knowledge. However, not everyone on the team has to have experience conducting research or have an in-depth knowledge of research methods. Having members on the team who have a research background as well as having members who have content knowledge (e.g., ELA or mathematics) is essential for creating a successful team.

DEVELOPING AN ACTION RESEARCH TEAM

Before any work can commence in Step One, an action research team must be formed. An **action research team** is a group of individuals who are responsible for overseeing and executing the collection, analysis, and interpretation of findings in order to address a school issue. The idea of a team that uses data to make curricular and school-level decisions is certainly becoming visible in our school culture today. Response to Intervention (RTI) and other models that employ such data teams are some examples of the importance of teams and their power to make real change in our schools. You also might know action research teams by other names, such as inquiry teams or data analysis teams. No matter what they are called, they all function similarly: They analyze data, identify problems or issues in the school that need to be addressed, and implement a method of treatment.

THE ROLE OF THE TEAM. A team is very important for setting the right context for the action research project. For example, the action research team can serve as a buffer between the school administrator and the data, the results, and the actions that are taken. If the school leader were to conduct all the steps of action research solo, the results of the action research would most likely not be fully embraced by staff, as in this chapter's vignette about Principal Tyler. Without a team, members of the school community might not understand the purpose of the intervention program and might come to the conclusion that it is "just" another project launched by the administration.

Remember that your attention, support, and vision as the school leader set the tone for the team and the degree of importance for the work the team will engage in within the school. Without your support and guidance, the team's work may be seen as peripheral, unimportant, and just another initiative that staff believes "will go away just like all the others" if they ignore it. But school-level action research teams will not go away. As the cornerstone for school improvement, their work is vitally important; therefore, the makeup of the team is critical to being able to successfully provide the right support for the activities in which they must engage.

Take a moment to read the following vignette.

Vignette 4.2
Creating Effective Action Research Teams

Sarah Tyler is a school leader at Abe Elementary where she has been a third-grade teacher for the past 15 years. Recently, the district announced that each school would form an action research team consisting of five or six teachers from the school. The team would meet once a week to examine school data.

Mrs. Tyler was appointed by her school principal, Mr. Francis, to serve as the lead on the school's data team. Excited by the challenge, Mrs. Tyler posted a notice in the office and sent a memo and e-mail around to the faculty asking for volunteers who would be willing to serve on the school's data team. She also provided a brief overview of members' responsibilities. Later that week she heard from several colleagues who were interested and signed up to serve on the data team. Initially, Mrs. Tyler was concerned that the teachers who volunteered were all relatively new (in their first 3 years teaching) and all from the third grade. Coming to the conclusion that "Beggars shouldn't be choosers," Mrs. Tyler decided that she should be thankful for the teachers who stepped up to serve on the team.

Mrs. Tyler spent the weekend before the first data team meeting pulling together district and school-level data from annual state assessments in mathematics and English language arts. She prepared the data and created formatted tables so members of the data team could clearly see the downward spiral over the last 5 years in student performance in mathematics at the fifth-grade level.

On Monday, Mrs. Tyler presented each member of the data team with a folder containing the data that she had assembled. Members opened their folders and began flipping through the pages of tables and charts.

After a few minutes Mrs. Tyler asked, "So what do you think about the data? What do you think it is telling us? What other types of data do we need to look at next?"

"Well," said one of the members, "this data certainly confirms what we already suspected—"

"That student performance on the state test really declines by the time students reach fifth grade," interjected another team member.

"Yeah, they really take a nosedive in fifth grade, don't they?" said another.

"So why do you think this is?" asked Mrs. Tyler, trying her best to facilitate the session. "What other types of data do we need now?"

"I don't think we need any more data," said another team member. She closed the folder and placed it in front of her.

"No more data?" asked Mrs. Tyler, surprised at what she had just heard. "Why not?"

"Well, the data confirmed what we already knew: that our students don't do well in fifth-grade mathematics," said yet another member. "But we're third-grade teachers. I don't have a clue what goes on in fifth grade, particularly in math."

"And we have only been here a few years. I don't even know what curriculum was being used in mathematics in the school five years ago," said another team member.

"Let's face it," chimed in another member, "you're going to have to get fifth-grade teachers on the team if you want to explore this data further."

Although there are no prescribed rules for who should be on an action research team, as the school leader there are some elements to consider for your school's team future and success. Overall, most effective action research teams have five to seven members. It is recommended that the team be a size that fits with the overall purpose of the action research project. The most important thing to remember is that you will not have enough perspective to make informed decisions if the team is too small. If the team is too big, the team may become too cumbersome to establish a focus and engage in meaningful work.

Although there is no magical formula for determining the most effective composition for an action research team, it is important to recognize that those individuals who make up the team should be selected purposefully. In other words, the team should be composed of individuals who have a unique set of skills, content knowledge, and experience. As the school leader, it is important for you to keep in mind that members on the team do not have to be stagnate. As depicted in Vignette 4.2, as team members begin to drill down and further examine data, new explorations present themselves. Because of this, new members may be added to the team at any time. In the vignette about school leader Mrs. Tyler, one possible next step would be to find fourth- and fifth-grade teachers to serve on the team to provide a more in-depth perspective of the situation at hand.

TYPES OF ACTION RESEARCH TEAMS

One possible model for an action research team is what is called a **single stakeholder-based team**. This group could be homogenously grouped, meaning it would include teachers from all of the same discipline (e.g., science or mathematics) or grade level (e.g., all third-grade teachers). However, you also could have a team that was heterogeneous or what is referred to as mixed panel. A **mixed-panel team** could include teachers as well as parents, members from the community, board members, and, in some cases, even student representatives. Despite the type of model you use for your team, the one thing to keep in mind is that your team members should be selected using purposeful sampling. This means that the members are not selected at random but, rather, because they express interest in doing such work and have perspective or expertise that will make them valuable to the team. See Figure 4.2 for an overview of the various types of action research teams.

When addressing issues surrounding instruction and assessment, it is important to select people who have in-depth knowledge not only of quality and rigorous instruction and content but also how it can be measured. For example, a speech and language pathologist might not necessarily be a school leader's first pick for working on literacy and ELA issues in the school; however, speech and language pathologists have in-depth and specific knowledge when it comes to measuring student improvements through intricate formative measures.

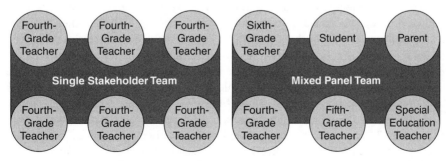

FIGURE 4.2 Types of Action Research Teams

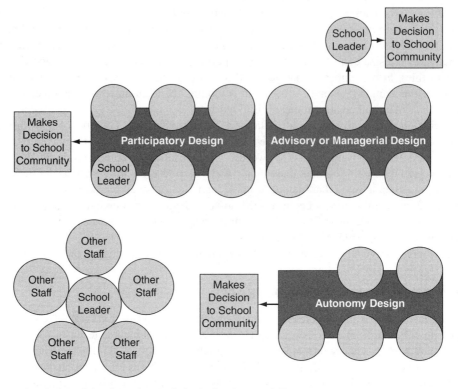

FIGURE 4.3 School Leader's Role in Action Research Team

In addition to deciding on the makeup of the action research team, it also is important for the school leader to determine the proximity to the action research team he or she wants to have. Figure 4.3 presents examples of designs for the role the school leaders will play in the action research process.

In the **participatory** design, the school leader plays an active role in all aspects of the action research process. In this design, the school leader will work closely with the other team members, engage in collecting and analyzing data, but only have "one voice" among the other voices of the team. One of the benefits of this design is that it certainly "diffuses" the school leader being a focal point in the action research process. In some cases, because of the climate of the school, a school leader may decide to use the **advisory/managerial design**. As you can see in Figure 4.3, the school leader does not sit "at the table" with the other action research members but, rather, sits out to the side. In this model, the action research team serves as an advisory committee. The action research team, which may be teacher based or a mixed panel, oversees the responsibilities of carrying out the action research steps. Periodic updates and any findings that are reported would be communicated to the school leader. The school leader would use this information to form or support the final decision. In most cases, the data and action research results should play into the school leader's decision, but ultimately it is "taken under advisement," as indicated by the arrows flowing in only one direction. The third design is what is referred to as **autonomy**. In this design, the school leader is very much removed from the work that the action research team is doing. The action research team reports out their updates and findings to the school leader, just like they would to the other school staff. In this design, the school leader plays no role in assisting the action research team with the scope and sequence of their work. The school leader's perspective or influence does not impact the team or the work that they are doing, thus giving the team complete autonomy to investigate the issue however it sees fit.

Summary

Although school-level and classroom-level action research have similar processes and are both designed to improve practice, school-level action research attempts to study a large impact, usually across an entire school. One distinct characteristic that separates the two types is the use of action research teams. Remember, as a school administrator and leader, one of your main roles is to foster relationships with staff and build community. The action research team is a unique and creative way to do just this by focusing and working on school-related issues. Successful action research teams do not happen by accident—they take considerable thought and planning. It is important to form the correct action research team to address the issue at hand. A team can consist of all fourth-grade teachers (e.g., single stakeholder-based teams) or a mixture of school staff, parents, and, in some cases, students (mixed panel teams). In addition to the composition of the action research teams, it also is important for school administrators and leaders to understand the relevance of their own position on or near the team. A participatory approach is when the administrator or leader sits directly on the action research team with only a single voice or vote on decisions that are made. In other situations, depending on the issues that are being addressed, the school administrator or leader may want to take an advisory/managerial approach. In this approach, the members of the action research team function separately *from* the school leader in making final recommendations for implementation and practice *to* the school leader. In this model, the school leader may accept or reject decisions made by the research team. Autonomy is similar to the advisory/managerial approach; however, in the autonomy model the administrator or school leader sits with the school staff but is removed from the action research or voicing anything about their ideas, decisions, or practices to solve the identified school issue.

Key Concepts

action research team
advisory/managerial design

autonomy
Level 2 school-level action research team

mixed panel team
participatory

single stakeholder-based team

Discussion/Reflection Question

1. This chapter presented the idea that a school administrator or leader could use an action research team to help foster relationships and build community within the school. If you were a school principal, how might you see an action research team in your school help you to accomplish this goal? Be sure to support your explanations for an upcoming class discussion.

Activities

1. Take a moment to reexamine the different roles or positions an administrator or school leader can take in an action research team (Figure 4.3). Review the descriptions for each of the various roles. Next generate at least one example of a school-level action research topic where these different roles or positions would be appropriate. Be sure you can support your reason for an upcoming class discussion.
2. Either individually or in a group, pick a school-level issue and design an action research team whose mission it is to address this issue. Who will be on your team? What will be their makeup and expertise? Why have you selected these individuals? Why will these individuals be able to come together to form the optimal research group? Also pretend that you are the school's principal. What would your role or position be in relation to the action research team? Why have you chosen this position for this particular topic? Develop your action research team description into a 10-minute presentation for the class.
3. Create a list of common positions found in a school (e.g., school psychologists, technology coordinator, school social worker, etc.). Next, for each individual position that you have listed, describe the expertise these individuals can contribute to the action research team.

CHAPTER 5

Analyzing Data as an Action Research Team

After reading this chapter you should be able to:

1. Understand the overall process of analyzing data to identify a problem or issue that needs to be addressed.
2. Understand the role and responsibility of the school leader and the action research team in analyzing school data.
3. Understand the benefits and limitations of the three main types of data that are available to action research teams.
4. Understand the four main methods for analyzing school archival data: disaggregation, trend, longitudinal/cohort, and concurrent validity.

Vignette 5.1
Data Analysis and the Action Research Team

The action research team at Mount St. Pierre Middle School was in the midst of examining the school's student performance data from the annual state assessment in English language arts (ELA). The team began by reviewing student performance on the state's ELA assessment for the past 5 years.

"Of grades six through eight, seventh grade has not performed as well as sixth or eighth across the past five years," noted one of the team members, a sixth-grade teacher.

"Do you have data on the other schools in the district?" asked Mrs. Smith, a seventh-grade mathematics teacher. "I am kind of curious to know how the other schools are doing. Is the same dip occurring in other seventh grades?"

"That's a good question," replied Mrs. Sanders, an instructional coach who is also serving as the school leader for the action research team. She then presented the data from two other middle schools in the district.

After analyzing these sets of data, the action research team determines that the same pattern of low performance is not occurring in seventh grade in the other middle schools in the district.

"Do we have an item analysis for the last five years for our seventh grade?" asked the school psychologist, another member of the team.

"That's another very good question," said Mrs. Sanders, and she directs the group to another page of data. These data provided the team with an aggregated overview of seventh-grade student performance by standards and items across the last 5 years.

The action research team then examined the next set of data and find that some patterns do exist; for example, seventh-grade students missed certain areas of the state assessment each year.

"When I look at the items students are missing," said Miss James, a seventh-grade ELA teacher, "I can see that this is material we typically cover in seventh grade at the end of the school year. We usually have to run through this material rather quickly at the end of the school year just before the test. Crunch time, I call it."

"Are these data available at an individual student level?" asked Mrs. Smith. "It would be helpful to be able to see which students didn't do well on these items, rather than having it aggregated by the entire grade level."

"Yes, it would be really helpful to know what students we are talking about," replied Miss James.

It took a lot of work, but at the next meeting Mrs. Sanders presented the data the action research team had requested. Action research team members began to sort the through individual student data by their incorrect and correct items on the state's ELA assessment for seventh grade within the past 5 years.

"What about students in seventh grade who did make the yearly benchmark?" asked Miss James. "What about those students? What do they look like?"

Having anticipated this, Mrs. Sanders provided members with this data. Team members then spent the next hour flipping through the individual reports for seventh-grade students by the types of items they missed. To Mrs. Sander's surprise, team members began to sort the report into piles: those students who had been successful on the state assessment (particularly for those items where teachers had said they had to crunch everything in before the test) and those students who had not been successful. Once they had sorted student reports into the two piles, team members had a discussion. They talked about interesting aspects of the data at this classroom level. They all took time to share their thoughts and perspectives.

"One thing that I started to notice as I sorted the data from last year was that many of the students who didn't do well on the assessment and missed the items concerning material we cover quickly at the end of the year, were students who I think miss a lot of school," said Miss James, the seventh-grade ELA teacher.

Mrs. Smith, the seventh-grade math teacher, replied, "Yes, as we were sorting last year's data, the names of the students were very familiar to me and what I remember about this unfortunately is that they missed a lot of school."

"Mrs. Sanders, can we also get student attendance data to go along with this data?" asked Miss James. "I think it would be very helpful in providing us a clearer picture of what we are looking at."

Mrs. Sanders agreed, and by the next action research meeting she had added the number of days absent, number of days tardy, and number of in-school and out-of-school suspensions to each of the students' reporting sheets. Now action research team members were able to examine those variables along with student performance on the state ELA assessment by type of items correct and incorrect for students who did and did not meet annual benchmarks. At the end of the action research meeting, members made an interesting discovery. They found that their hypothesis had been confirmed: Students who had higher rates of absenteeism and missed proportionally more of the items that teachers said they had to crunch in order to cover the material before the annual state assessment.

But action research team members did not stop there.

At the next meeting Mrs. Smith asked, "Could we possibly get the absenteeism and in- and out-of-school suspension data for the students who did not perform to benchmark on the state assessment by date?"

Mrs. Sanders said that she didn't see why not and, as always, at the next meeting she provided the team with the data by date.

At this micro level of data analysis, action team members made another very interesting discovery. They found that students who were missing the majority of the "end-of-year items on the ELA assessment missed more days and were suspended (both in and out of school) more than students who met benchmark and didn't miss these items. Even more interesting was the fact that when the action research team analyzed the attendance and suspension data by the actual dates in the school year, they found that these students tended to miss more days of school and/or have their in- and out-of-school suspensions *at the end of the school year*, coinciding perfectly with the test preparation crunch.

Excited by this discovery, members of the action research team began to plan an intervention about how to address this issue. They immediately had a meeting with the school principal, the dean of school suspension, and the head of the district's truancy office to work on a plan to decrease student absenteeism and redirect student suspensions during this critical test preparation time.

HOW TO ANALYZE DATA AS AN ACTION RESEARCH TEAM

Once your action research team has been established, the next step is to conduct an analysis of the school's data. This process is often referred to as **data-based decision making** and is a process that is used to determine what area or issue needs to be addressed in the school. In some cases, as in Vignette 5.1, the analysis can also shine some light on the matter and give way to support some possible solutions that the action research team may want to implement to correct the situation.

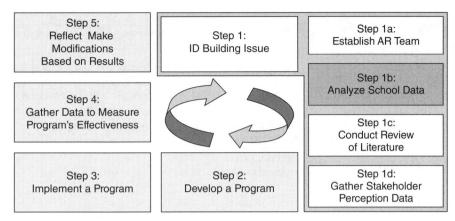

FIGURE 5.1 Steps in School-Level Action Research

Although collecting in-depth data are a critical element, all too often members of a school will skip the needs assessment step because they believe that they already know what the problem and its cause are. By doing so, the action research team may not be building its eventual program on a solid foundation. A comprehensive, well-conducted analysis of all available data will help the action research team clearly identify a school-level issue and help lead team members along the path of figuring out what intervention or program can be implemented to best address it.

THREE MAIN DATA POINTS FOR NEEDS ASSESSMENT: AN OVERVIEW

For the purposes of this book, the **needs assessment** is divided into the collection and analysis of three different types of data:

- School archival data
- Data from past research and literature (promising or effective practices)
- Staff feedback or stakeholder-based perception data

In addition, this chapter will describe the needs assessment process, as well as the three different types of data, how they should be analyzed, and how to bring all the data together to truly make a data-based decision.

School Archival Data

Experts such as Bernhardt (2000) and Stiggins and Duke (2008) tell us that there is no lack of data in our schools today. In fact, over the last decade schools have quickly become one of the richest sources of data, requiring warehouses and massive database systems to help organize and manage it all. Unfortunately, some experts also believe that schools today have too much data, making it difficult for administrators, teachers, and related staff members to focus on what data should be critically examined and what issues need to be addressed first (Bernhardt).

If you think about it, data are being collected every second in school districts, schools, and classrooms. These data are used, or should be used, for different purposes. Students arrive at school and the attendance role is taken, students take a quiz at the end of a lesson, students take

Table 5.1 Three Types of School Archival Data

Type of School Archives	Classroom-Level Data	School/Program-Level Data	Institutional/Policy-Level Data
Student Academic	Student Quizzes Grades Homework Chapter Tests Unit Tests Student Projects	Student performance on program measures, district benchmarks Student grade reading levels	Student performance on annual state assessments Standardized measures
Student Behavioral	Classroom Behavior	Attendance Tardiness	Dropout
School Demographics			Teacher Turnover Rate % Teachers Teaching Out of Certification % Teachers with a Master's Degree

a unit test at the end of their unit on matter in science, and so forth. In addition, the amount of data may be self-defeating (see Table 5.1, which presents broad categories and examples of just some of the data found in school systems).

INSTITUTIONAL/POLICY LEVEL DATA. School officials are used to working with systems accountability data (see Table 5.1). This type of data is typically generated from standardized assessments that students take annually in key content areas (e.g., ELA or mathematics). Low student performance on systems accountability data will place a school or district on an in-need-of-improvement list. Experts, such as Stiggins and Duke (2008), report that although systems accountability data are used to evaluate the effectiveness of school administrators; however, they are not the sole source of data a school administrator should examine if he or she wants to improve a low-performing school. In Vignette 5.1, the action research team initially examined instructional/policy-level data when they reviewed student performance on the state's annual ELA assessments; however, on further examination you will also note that the action research did not stop there. The team continued to question and further examine school-level data in an attempt to acquire a better understanding of the situation at hand.

SCHOOL/PROGRAM-LEVEL DATA. Aside from data derived from state accountability testing, schools themselves produce many different types of data. Schools administer many standardized assessments on their own accord. It is important to note that data from these assessments is not reported to the state but, rather, is kept internally within the school and typically used by school officials for progress monitoring of students as well as to gauge and evaluate programming.

CLASSROOM-LEVEL DATA. These data on student performance in the classroom can be collected daily, weekly, monthly, or quarterly. The scope is virtually unlimited and typically includes both formative and summative data. Examples of these types of data include, but are not limited to, daily quizzes, student homework, choral responses, student group work, student projects, chapter tests, and unit tests. Experts in the field believe that these are the most important data for helping school administrators improve their schools and increase student performance on both school/program assessments and systems accountability assessments.

ANALYSIS TECHNIQUES

The four main methods for analyzing school archival data are disaggregation, trend, longitudinal/cohort, and concurrent validity analysis. These techniques can be used on all three types of data (i.e., systems, program, and classroom); however, as noted by Stiggins and Duke (2008), these analysis techniques are primarily focused on systems accountability data. They can (and should) be used, however, across all three types of school archival data.

ESTABLISHING A BASELINE. **Baseline** is a term that you may have heard before. It is important that baseline data be examined as part of the process. Baseline data will provide a more accurate picture as to what is occurring or has already occurred (Lodico, Spaulding, & Voegtle, 2010). Take for example, 2 years of office referral data for School A. In 2006–07, School A reported 223 total office referrals for the school year. The following year (2007–08), the total number of referrals was 99. What might one conclude from this data snapshot? Most likely, one would conclude that the school has had a dramatic decrease in office referrals. Perhaps, it was the implementation of a new program in the classrooms to address problem behavior, or a change in school policy as to what constitutes an office referral; there is a whole host of possible explanations as to why this happened. Pretend that more data were available on School A. In 2005–06, there were 90 office referrals, and in 2004–05 there were 95. Now, does this additional information shed a new light on the situation and your interpretation? Probably. These new data provide a wider window in which to view more of the school's office referral data. With the additional data you can now see that the 2006–07 data (223 referrals) constituted an anomaly or movement from an established pattern. Going back and examining several years of archival data prior to introducing the treatment or program is referred to as baseline data. How far back in the data should you go to establish baseline? Although there are no set rules as to how many years consist of a rigorous baseline, it is recommended that you collect and analyze at least 3 years of data so you are comfortable that this pattern exists in your school and is not some random occurrence.

DISAGGREGATION ANALYSIS. One of the most common data analysis techniques is searching for a gap in the data (Goldring & Berends, 2009). A gap is essentially what it sounds like: a blip in the spread of the data where something looks quite different from what it should—in other words, it is something that needs to be addressed and approved on. However, although school data sets are filled with items that need to be improved, essentially someone (e.g., teachers, the school leader, a group of school officials) must examine the data and deem the gap unacceptable. School action plans are focused on addressing these gaps in the data.

One common gap found in many schools' data is the gap in student performance on standardized assessments (e.g., in ELA or mathematics). In some cases, the gap can be found when examining the entire school or across grade levels—for example, only 37% of eighth-graders passing the state's ELA assessment on a given year. Or the gap may require those conducting the analysis to compare the achievement of different subgroups or subcategories for students' performance. Table 5.2 illustrates the percentage of eighth-grade students passing the state's ELA assessment in fictional School A for the last 4 years. In examining the ELA data, what do you conclude?

Table 5.2 Percentage of Eighth-Graders Passing State ELA Assessment

2002–03	2003–04	2004–05	2005–06
91%	88%	90%	90%

$N = 286$ students.

You probably concluded that eighth-graders in School A have been doing well on the state assessment. After all, roughly 90% of students have consistently passed the assessment. However, if you begin to disaggregate the data by subgroups of students (e.g., ethnicity, free or reduced lunch, and days absent) you begin to see a different picture emerging (see Table 5.3 for the data organized by ethnicity for the roughly 10% of students not performing to the standard).

This new analysis certainly does not resemble findings from the first set of data. The second analysis clearly shows a gap in the performance of African American eighth-graders on the state assessment. In fact, African American males make up approximately 99% of the students not performing to the standard on the assessment. Keep in mind that the analysis does not conclude that all students who are African American are not passing that state assessment. It does indicate, however, that of the subpopulation of students in School A who are not passing the state's ELA assessment each year for eighth grade, almost all are African American. Although the action research team at School A will need to conduct further analysis to see if this pattern also is occurring at other grades, they certainly do not need to look any further than this one data point to begin to start their quest to improve student performance.

Another element to keep in mind is that this data analysis process is primarily diagnostic in nature, meaning that it highlights or identifies the issue or problem in the data. However, it does not draw cause–effect relationships to answer *why* the gap has occurred in the first place. There are ways to go about examining other possible variables to get a better or tighter picture of the situation at hand. For example, you and your school's action research team might ask these questions: What is the attendance for the 10% of students not passing the state ELA assessment? Is the real issue here quality of instruction or students not attending school? These are important and logical questions to ask. Without them, one might make the assumption that the issue is

Table 5.3 Subgroup Analysis of Eighth Grade ELA Assessment Data: Students Not Performing to the Standard

	2002–03	2003–04	2004–05	2005–06
White	0%	0%	0%	0%
Black or African American	9%	11%	10%	10%
Hispanic or Latino	0%	1%	0%	0%
Asian or Native Hawaiian/Other Pacific Islander	0%	0%	0%	0%

instructional, perhaps failing to provide appropriate or differentiated instruction to students. However, if school attendance is the real issue then the treatment or program would be dramatically shifted in order to address the problem.

After examining the latest set of data, the school principal and members of the action research team conclude that their first order of business is to address the high absenteeism of these students. Now suppose that the action research team made a startling, yet increasingly common discovery when examining student attendance. Suppose the team found that across the eighth grade, not just African American male students but also eighth-grade students in general had relatively lower attendance rates than, let's say, student in seventh grade or sixth grade in the same school or another middle school in the district. Students overall were missing a lot of school, but somehow the other subgroups of students were able to perform well on the state assessment and meet the required benchmark. How would this new finding play into better understanding the problem? Have these new data changed the way you had previously viewed or interpreted the situation?

In some situations, it is impossible through the disaggregation of the data to determine a cause–effect relationship. In many cases, it eventually boils down to an educated guess on the part of the action research team.

TREND ANALYSIS. Trend analysis is another common analysis technique (Goldring & Berends, 2009). **Trend analysis** data are examined at one point in time across multiple years. In Table 5.2, examining eighth graders' scores on the ELA for 4 years in a row is an example of trend analysis. The one thing to keep in mind when examining data using a trend analysis is that you are looking at different cohorts or groups of students each year. Therefore, in the preceding example, the data are based not on the same students year after year but on different eighth-graders. It is important to recognize that the students are different each year; therefore, if performance is consistently low (i.e., a trend) in eighth-graders, it does have some consistency but not because of some trait exhibited by the group itself.

LONGITUDINAL OR COHORT ANALYSIS. This is another technique whereby data are consistently monitored for a set sample or group of individuals (Goldring & Berends, 2009). An example of this would be to go back to the sixth grade and track the performance on ELA assessments for the students now in eighth grade. This particular analysis is important for devising a story with context about these students by providing data from their past. Perhaps, in the case of the eighth-graders not passing the state assessment, it is evident that it started back in the sixth grade and that these students have continually been passed through the grades without meeting the standards on the state assessment but passing ELA on their report cards. It is important to keep in mind with the longitudinal analysis that the data are only telling the story for one group. In some cases, this may be what is referred to as a rogue class, and their performance over time may have been very different from that of other classes moving through the system; this would be something that one would want to check when analyzing the data. This would be the case with the data in Table 5.2, which consistently showed 10% of eighth-grade students not passing the ELA assessment on an annual basis. A longitudinal analysis for each one of those classes from 2002–03 to 2005–06 should be examined back to the sixth grade to see if they exhibit the same pattern. As you can begin to see from the preceding examples, the more exploration one does with the data, the more questions begin to emerge and the more in-depth perspective one develops.

CONCURRENT VALIDITY ANALYSIS. This analysis stems from the concurrent validity practice of standardized measures discussed in Chapter 12.

In **concurrent validity analysis** the action research team examines student performance on two different standardized measures as a way of establishing a more in-depth understanding of the data (as well as the measures) and what the real issues are (Bernhardt, 2000). Let's take School A. Remember the approximately 90% of students who were passing the state's annual assessment in ELA? From an earlier analysis, we deemed that overall the school was doing well, right? Well, let's say you conduct a more in-depth analysis of what this really means by comparing students' scores on the standardized state assessments to another score related to ELA. In this case, let's examine students' reading levels.

Reading levels are a common measure established for students and are particularly important for determining a student's reading grade level. As you likely would think, research on reading levels and student success in school show the two to be highly correlated with one another. Therefore, when the action research team examined the 90% of eighth-grade students who passed the state assessment in ELA, they were surprised to find that 30% of those students were not on grade level for reading. In fact, most were two to three grade levels below. What does this type of finding tell you in relation to preparing the students for future success in the real world? A further discussion of this issue can be found in the Chapter 5 on measuring outcomes.

Summary

Level 2 action research is unique in that it focuses on making schoolwide impact and uses an action research team approach to do so. One of the key initial steps in Level 2 action research is the needs assessment. In performing an assessment, three types of data are examined: school archival, staff and stakeholder feedback, and past research/literature. All three of these data points are then triangulated or brought together to serve as a platform for the action research team to decide what treatment or program to select and put in place to address the issue.

In addition it is important for the action research team to examine current school data. A wide variety of data analysis techniques can be used to analyze these data. These include disaggregation, trend, longitudinal/cohort, and concurrent validity analysis.

Key Concepts

baseline
concurrent validity analysis
longitudinal or cohort analysis
needs assessment
trend analysis

Discussion/Reflection Question

1. Whether you are currently a school administrator or will be one in the near future, what are some problems or issues that you think you would like to address in your school? What types of data would you and your action research team examine as part of the needs assessment?

Activities

1. Pretend you are a school leader on an action research team responsible along with the other members for analyzing the ELA data for the past 4 years for eighth-grade students. What might be your response following your examining of the data in Table 5.2? Then what might be your prognosis following examination of the data in Table 5.3? How are those two analyses different?

2. Pick a topic or issue that as a school leader you feel needs to be addressed to ensure ongoing school improvement. Review the current research and literature on the topic. Gather five to ten articles on the topic, review them, and be prepared to share with the class what you have learned from this process.

CHAPTER 6

Examining Past Research, and Reviewing and Critiquing Cause–Effect Experimental Research

After reading this chapter you should be able to:

1. Understand the main purpose for conducting a review of the literature.
2. Identify the different types of documents that constitute the literature on a topic.
3. Understand the key search engines and databases that are available for searching the literature.
4. Understand how an action research team can work collaboratively to conduct a review of the literature.
5. Distinguish between the three different types of cause–effect research: experimental, quasi-experimental, and causal–comparative.
6. Understand the key criteria when critiquing cause–effect research.

Vignette 6.1
Analyzing Data

After examining student behavioral data, the data team at Metro Middle School determined the need to implement a behavior program in the school. The next question asked by team members was, What behavior program should we implement and what program is most effective for addressing student behavior issues schoolwide?

The next step taken by the action research team was to begin to explore the literature and past research on behavior programs. The team found that there was no shortage of articles or literature on schoolwide behavior programs. In addition, the action research team had no difficulty sorting the literature into two piles: research and non-research; however, team members discovered that sorting the research pile into different types of research was indeed a challenge. What they found to be even more of a challenge was determining if a study that examined the effectiveness of a program or intervention was indeed rigorous.

"I think this research study was a quality study because there was a treatment and control group and the students were randomly assigned to those groups to receive the behavior program," said Mr. Finch, an eighth-grade science teacher.

"I agree. When I was going through the studies I only came across the same one," said Miss James, the sixth-grade ELA teacher. "Putting the ethical issues aside, I'm not sure how that program would work in our school. Would we find the same results?"

"That's the problem with a lot of research," said Mrs. Jennings. "A study might show that something is successful, but when you roll it out in another school you don't get the same results."

"I think that many time researchers have an agenda and use data to drive that agenda," said another team member.

"I agree," said Mr. Finch. "Whenever I hear the words 'research says,' I say to myself, 'Okay, here it comes.'"

"I feel the same way," replied Mrs. Jennings. "Researchers can get research to say anything that they want it to say, so why should we rely so much on what research *says*?"

"Plus, I don't know about all of you, but it's been awhile since I took a research course," said Mr. Franklin, who taught social studies. "And I can't recall all there is about how to critique a research study, particularly one that looks at cause and effect."

"I feel the same way," said Miss Finch. "I remember that there is a treatment and control, but I am not sure if I could really critique a study like this from what I remember."

While taking notes during the discussion, one thing became clear to Mrs. Jackson, the team's leader: She was going to have to work with the action research team and provide some professional development and readings on the different research approaches and how to critique research studies that focused on making cause–effect inferences. She knew she had her work cut out for her.

EXAMINING PAST RESEARCH AND LITERATURE

In addition to the school archival data, the action research team should also review the current literature on the topic or issue, as well as all possible solutions that have sound research behind them.

The following are some questions that should be answered as part of the action research team's examination of past research and literature on a topic or issue:

- What does past research say about the issue or problem identified in the school?
- Do any research-based interventions or programs address the specific issue or problem the action research team has identified?
- What, if any, challenges or barriers to the programs or interventions are noted in the research? If any, what are they and how might you this information be used when deciding on an approach to take?

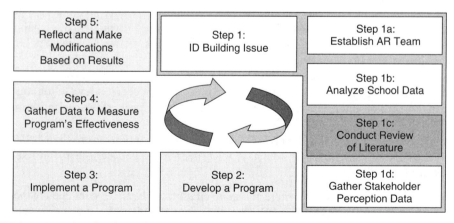

FIGURE 6.1 Steps in School-Level Action Research Process

Consulting the review of literature and analyzing past research has been traditionally a step conducted by professional researchers. In Chapter 2 of this book you read about some of the reasons why school administrators are apprehensive about using research to select curriculum or educational interventions or programs. Despite this, it is still imperative that you, the school leader, and members of the action research team review the literature. One of the main reasons researchers conduct a review of the literature is so they have a solid and strong rationale for conducting their study. The same holds true for the action research team. The team uses past research to help provide a framework for its investigations and to make the most data-based decisions possible in working to address the identified school issue or problem.

Although action research certainly acknowledges the importance of conducting a review of literature, it has to take into account certain context that researchers may not be subjected to. First of all, it has to take into account the climate of the school. In other words, it has to be responsive to what the current school culture (e.g., teachers and staff) believes. Although research may point in one direction, the current perspective among staff may be pointed in the opposite direction. To bring in a treatment or program that is counterintuitive to the school's current climate might be detrimental in the fact that teachers and staff might not fully implement the treatment. These are all important elements that the action research team members need to consider when reviewing the literature.

DATABASES

The first step that needs to be conducted when reviewing the literature is to access research journals and databases. In Chapter 2, peer-reviewed journals and scholarly journals were discussed, along with their role in providing rigorous research to inform practice. In addition, academic databases should also be examined. The following constitutes a brief overview of some common databases:

- The **Educational Resources Information Center (ERIC)** is perhaps the most common database. It exists at most large public libraries and universities. At the very least a school leader should have access to the ERIC database and use it regularly to research issues and topics necessary for decision making. ERIC is not a journal, nor is it peer reviewed. ERIC is a clearinghouse, meaning that it publishes materials and research that has been submitted by individuals. ERIC uses no editing process and no review of methods or approaches. Although there may be items on ERIC that are not rigorous, researchers often publish their research presentations from important conferences in ERIC before seeking to publish them in a scholarly or peer-reviewed journal.
- Another popular database, **PsycINFO**, contains scholarly articles, book chapters, books, and dissertations. PsycINFO is one resource that contains peer-reviewed literature. More than 2.5 million citations date all the way back to the early 1800s, with international offerings.
- Similar to PsycINFO, the **PsycARTICLES** database contains more than 140,000 references from more than 60 journals with peer-reviewed scholarly and scientific research.

With advances in technology, more and more citations and articles contained in these databases are available in full text, in either PDF or HTML format. This makes collection and analysis of studies and literature a bit easier, and certainly more time efficient for busy members of a school's action research team.

SELECTING FROM THE REVIEW OF LITERATURE

When we use the word "**literature**" we are actually referring to a larger collection of different types of materials relating to a topic. The term *literature* encompasses empirical research studies, reviews of literature and past research, theoretical pieces, opinion pieces, and how-to/practitioner-oriented articles (see Figure 6.2).

Empirical research is a term used to refer to research studies. Although the term *research study* is used in a broad sense, technically the process has to follow a series of steps in order to be called research. A complete description of these steps can be found in Chapter 2; however, the following are the basic components for research listed:

1. A question is asked or a hypothesis is generated.
2. Data are collected (quantitative or qualitative data).
3. Data are analyzed.
4. Results are generated.
5. Implications are made for practice and future research.

As you and your action research team begin to sort through the literature, you will need to come up with a method for organizing and extracting the important information out of each source. Although there is no right method for how to go about doing this, certainly some strategies are more effective than others. You might want to try some of the following strategies:

- Avoid printing everything that you come in contact with.
- Try to determine what type of article you are looking at: an empirical research study, a theoretical piece, a practitioner how-to piece, or an opinion piece. A research study will have certain components or section: a purpose statement, research questions or a hypothesis, a sample section, procedures, results, and discussion.
- Keep track of the exact words and terms you use when searching the research databases. When your action research team members disburse and begin to conduct their literature search, be sure that everyone keeps track of the key words and the various combinations of those key words that they have used. You will see that you don't have to get far into it before you start asking yourself the question, Did I already search using that key word? Therefore, it is highly recommended that key words be established and a list of specific

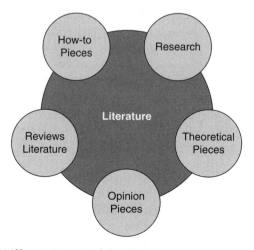

FIGURE 6.2 Overview of Different Aspects of the Literature

> ### BOX 6.1 Example of an Abstract
>
> Middle school students often experience many challenges when learning mathematics. Making math real, as well as implementing differentiated lessons, have certainly been, in many ways, a focus on current math instruction. The purpose of this study was to examine the effects of using manipulatives in a sixth-grade mathematics classroom to increase student learning. Thirty students were randomly assigned to receive 10 weeks of math class using various math manipulatives. In addition, 30 other students were randomly assigned to receive traditional mathematics instruction, using direct instruction by the teacher with no manipulatives. Students who received manipulatives had a significant increase in performance on a unit exam over those students in the control group. This study identifies implications for practices.

key words be distributed to the action research team members. After an initial search, the team members reconvene, share their results, determine if they need more, and devise the next set of key word searches. Ideally, this process would continue until the team members feel they have enough literature on the topic to move forward.

- Initially skim the research articles and literature as a screening technique before you sit down and read them from beginning to end. You will save a lot of time that way.
- Use the **abstracts** of research articles to get a better understanding of the complete study. The abstract is a 150- to 250-word summary of a research article. If a study contains an abstract, it usually appears right after the article's title and authors. Abstracts are beneficial because they essentially summarize an entire study in a small number of words. Take a moment to examine the abstract in Box 6.1. What can you quickly learn about this study?
- Find the study's purpose statement as soon as possible. It can usually be found in the first few paragraphs.
- Find the study's research questions and/or hypothesis. A quality study should have one or more overarching research questions. Research questions will be clearly labeled and will serve as the guiding framework for the researcher. Also, if you continued to read through the study you would notice that the results section of the study will repeat those research questions again and specifically answer those questions through the analysis of the study's results. Not all studies are required to have a hypothesis. A **hypothesis** is essentially a prediction that the researcher makes at the beginning of the study. The research bases this hypothesis on the results of past research, past experience, and theory and collects and analyzes data to determine if the results support or do not support a hypothesis. Notice, that we didn't say "prove" a hypothesis. Saying one is going to prove a hypothesis is considered to be bias in the scientific process. Scientists collect data and then analyze their data as a separate process.
- Determine as soon as possible what the variables and treatments (if any) in the study were.
- Examine the population or sample section to determine if the setting is similar to your own.
- Establish the main instruments or measures that were used in the study.
- Establish a basic framework for the procedures used to deliver treatments (if applicable) and gather data.

FULL TEXT AND HTML

Today's technological age certainly makes accessing electronic information a lot easier than it was 10 or 20 years ago. No longer do you have to make notations on index cards and spend hours in the library flipping through the card catalog. In fact, it is highly possible to conduct a thorough review of the literature and never even set foot in a library.

Although this is certainly convenient for busy school leaders and members of the action research team, one strategy that is not effective (or efficient) is to automatically print a hard copy of every document that you encounter. If you do so, you will be overrun with materials to read and sort through, and you will waste a lot of paper. The first strategy that you and members of the team should employ is using the abstracts for each paper. The abstract is a 150- to 250-word or less summary of the study or the purpose of the paper. Reviewing the abstract should tell you everything there is to know about the paper. If it sounds promising then the paper might be worth keeping; however, you should check out a few more sections before deciding on adding it to your pile for further review.

The next question you want to ask yourself is, Is this article an empirical research study, a theoretical piece, a practitioner piece, or an op-ed piece? Although there could be overlap among these four categories, it is important to be able to categorize them as much as possible. If the study is indeed an empirical research study, you will want to examine the different sections of the research.

In addition, you will want to take what you have learned about quantitative and qualitative research and what makes for a rigorous study and apply it to critiquing the empirical research that you have found on the topic or issue. Remember, just because something is published (even in a peer-reviewed journal) doesn't automatically make it a rigorous or quality study (even though it certainly helps). Ultimately, you, your staff, and your students are the end users or consumer of this research, and therefore it needs to be critiqued by you. If it is deemed rigorous and valuable then it should be added to the keep pile and used as a data point in the needs assessment process.

THE ACTION RESEARCH TEAM AND THE REVIEW OF LITERATURE

Do you remember the old saying "Two hands are better than one?" This couldn't be more true when reviewing the literature on a school issue using an action research team. If an action research team is made up of five individuals and every individual reviews five studies or articles, the team would have a total of 25 citations reviewed as part of their research efforts. Reviewing this amount of literature will give your action research team (as well as your project) a significant advantage when trying to generate possible solutions to addressing your school's issues or problems.

As you read in Chapter 2, school administrators have historically not trusted research or their findings in making schoolwide decisions. The important thing to keep in mind is that this is a collective process and that the results of one study should not drive a decision to implement a certain treatment or program. All the research that you uncover and piece together paints a picture: a pattern for you and your action research team to use as a platform (along with school archival data and staff or stakeholder feedback) to make your final decision.

ANALYZING THE REVIEW OF LITERATURE

The next thing you will need to think about is how to go about organizing and critiquing the research and other artifacts you come across in reviewing the literature. Before you begin to read how to critique the different types of research that you will encounter, it is important to have some strategies in place or a plan for how to assemble and use the research that you are about to gather.

One strategy used by both new and experienced researchers is an article summary sheet. An article summary sheet is essentially a graphic organizer. Although your action research team can certainly design its own, an example of a basic article summary sheet can be found in

> **EXHIBIT 6.1** **Example of an Article Summary Sheet**
>
> **Title:**
>
> **Author:**
>
> **Journal:**
>
> **Year:**
>
> **Vol. # Issue #**
>
> **Electronic Tag:**
>
> **Type of Source**
>
> __ Journal Article __ Paper presented at Conference __ Book or Book Chapter
> __ Technical Report __ Government Document __ Web site
> __ Other (please describe)
>
> **Type of Study (List Type of Study):**
>
> **Purpose:**
>
> **Research Questions/Hypothesis:**
>
> **Sample:**
>
> **Procedure:**
>
> **Summary of Findings:**
>
> **Critique:**

Exhibit 6.1. Although article summary sheets can vary depending on the scope of the project, they are highly recommended by experts in the field to those relatively new to research (Lodico, Spaulding, & Voegtle, 2010).

The purpose of the article summary sheet is to provide you and your action research team with a framework for extrapolating and summarizing key pieces of information from the study or article. The last thing members of the action research team would want to do when compiling their report or making a presentation to the school staff would be to go back and reread all the literature that they had collected. Instead, the article summary sheets serve as an index that makes it easier to retrieve and organize information. It is recommended that an article summary sheet be completed for every study or article collected by the action research team. Since not everything the action research team collects will be research, we have created a literature matrix, a second type of summary sheet. This sheet can be used for more general purposes and for articles that are not based on research.

CREATING A LITERATURE MATRIX

Once the action research team has gathered all the literature and created article summary sheets, the next step is to step back to analyze and summarize across all the studies and articles. An effective technique to use is the literature matrix (Mills, 2010). Although it may sound difficult, the literature

EXHIBIT 6.2 Example of a Literature Matrix

Topic: Technology Integration in the Classroom

Author	Year	Teacher Efficacy and Use of Technology	Challenges to Technology Integration in Education	Changing Teacher Practices	Best Method of PD and Tech.	Types of Technology Teachers Use
Abbey & Smith	2008	X	X	X		X
Brady	2002		X		X	
Davidson & Jones	2009	X		X	X	
Frank & Sanders	2006		X		X	X
Hooper & Brown	2010	X	X		X	X
Jones	2011	X	X		X	X
Smith & Snyder	2009	X	X	X		

matrix is actually a table that summarizes each study or article by the variables each examined. Exhibit 6.2 presents an example of a literature matrix for a literature review on school suspension.

In the first column the action research team has listed the authors for each of the 10 articles they have received. In the next column they have indicated the year of publication for each of the articles. Articles in the matrix can either be arranged alphabetically by the last name of the first author or by publication date, depending on how the action research team wants to analyze the matrix when it is completed. In the next columns the action research team has delineated different variables. These variables or themes are the major components that school suspension research and literature address. The action research team also has indicated which variables are focused on for each study or article. As you examine the literature matrix you can easily see which variables are examined or discussed throughout and which are only highlighted a couple of times.

Developing a literature matrix is also recommended as an activity that the action research team should do together. It is not something that a school administrator should be doing and then presenting to the action research team. It is intended to be a collaborative project during which team members not only come together to share and discuss but also to learn about the issue that they are working on and to begin thinking about possible strategies and programs that can be implemented.

HOW TO CRITIQUE CAUSE–EFFECT RESEARCH

One of the first questions asked by school leaders and educators when they begin gathering research and examining the literature is., Is this study a quality study? Although this question may seem simplistic, it is actually quite complex—after all, what criteria would one use in determining quality of research methods? Over the course of the next several chapters we highlight the main types of quantitative and qualitative research, provide an overview of their methodologies, and provide key criteria for you and your action research team members to think about when critiquing these types of research studies during your review of literature.

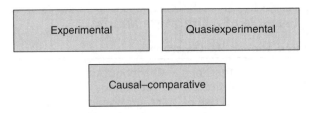

FIGURE 6.3 Three Types of Cause–Effect Research

As an administrator or school leader, it is important to know what works. During a given school day only so much learning time is available, and with today's emphasis on accountability there is no time to waste on instruction that is ineffective. Experimental, quasi-experimental, and causal–comparative research all attempt to answer the research question, What works? (See Figure 6.3.)

In the remainder of this chapter you will learn more about these three approaches, how they vary in their ability to answer the question "What Works?", and what their benefits and challenges are. One main characteristic that separates these three types of cause–effect research is how the participants (or subjects, as they are often referred to) are selected.

EXPERIMENTAL RESEARCH

As previously noted, there are many different types of research—each with a unique purpose, perspective, and set of methods. Although all these types of research are important, perhaps none is more important to school leaders than experimental research. In **experimental research**, participants are randomly selected from a population and then randomly assigned to treatment and control groups (see Figure 6.4). **Randomization** is a process used by researchers to select individuals from a population whereby each individual in the population has an *equal* chance of being selected for the study and where an individual being selected *does not interfere* with someone else being selected.

Following random selection, participants are randomly assigned to a treatment or a control group. The treatment group is the group that receives the variable being studied. In most cases, this would be the new variable the researcher hypothesizes would account for a significant increase in improvement in student performance when compared to the other variable presented in the control group. Participants in a control group receive no treatment. Since it is impossible in education to have students sitting around twiddling their thumbs for a control

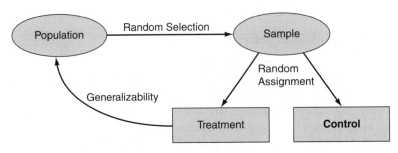

FIGURE 6.4 Overview of Randomization Process for Experimental Research

group experience, they are often exposed to study hall or any other course offering as long as it doesn't compete with, or have any connection to, the variable delivered in the treatment group. For example, if students in the treatment group are receiving a new reading intervention because they are struggling readers, then students in the control group cannot be using the time to work on reading skills with a tutor or instructional coach. In other words, students in the control group should not be using the control group class time to do anything related directly or indirectly to literacy and reading assistance.

HOW SHOULD ACTION RESEARCH TEAMS CRITIQUE EXPERIMENTAL RESEARCH?

As depicted in the scenario at the beginning of this chapter, understanding experimental research is a key component in being able to use it to guide an action research team in selecting the most promising practice to address the situation or issue that has been revealed through the process of data analysis. However, many administrators realize that findings from an experimental study might not necessarily be the same for their schools. Researchers refer to this as the study's external validity or its generalizability. Ideally researchers would like the results from their studies to generalize back to the larger population from which they were randomly selected, as shown in Figure 6.4. Since the study used a sample that was drawn randomly from the larger population, the research would likely say that the study's results were good for or generalizable to the larger population. In other words, if the study had used an entire population the same results would have been found.

Although researchers would like to have as large a population as possible to generalize back to, in reality such gross generalizability of studies is often compromised by how the study is conducted. Although members of an action research team may not all be experts in experimental research design, there are some commonsense components that everyone (experienced to naive) can easily look for when examining experimental research.

Length of Exposure to Treatment

How much time were students exposed to the treatment in the study?

Does this length of time match the time students would regularly spend in a classroom with this treatment?

Experimental research can be conducted in two different places. It can be conducted in actual classrooms in actual schools with students, or it can be conducted in a laboratory-like setting. In both cases, it is important for the action research to ascertain how much treatment students were exposed to and, more important, did this exposure match the amount of time students would be exposed to the same treatment during a school day. For example, a study during which students were randomly assigned to 90 minutes per day of a treatment (let's say a reading intervention) for 5 days a week for the entire school year showed that these students made significant gains in reading over those students in the control group. Great! However, how closely does the 90 minutes for 5 days a week match the amount of time that could be spent on a reading intervention? After all, other subjects and activities take up the school day. If a school could realistically only spend 45 to 50 minutes (roughly one period a day) on such an intervention for those students who needed it, the school would most likely not find the same results from the reading intervention as the researcher did in the experimental study. Infusing the reading inventory into the ELA classroom 5 minutes here and 15 minutes there will not result in the same gains as supported by the study. Matching the amount of time students will have to engage in a treatment to the real school day is something that members of the action research team must carefully consider before deciding to adopt a program or intervention based solely on research.

Who Delivers the Treatment?

Who delivers the treatment in the study?

How was that individual selected?

What are the characteristics of the person delivering the treatment? Do these characteristics differ from those of most of the staff in your school?

Aside from how much time is allotted to the treatment in a study, school leaders and members of the action research team should also be aware of who is delivering the treatment in the study. In many educational research studies (particularly those that take place in real classrooms), a teacher is usually the one to deliver the treatment, whether it is a reading intervention, an instructional strategy, or a classroom management plan. In many of these studies the participants (i.e., students) are randomly selected and assigned to treatment and control groups, but oftentimes those administering the treatment are not. It many cases a teacher or teachers are hand selected by the researcher or the school administrator because that person contains a unique set of qualities or characteristics that make them the ideal candidate to implement the treatment. It is understakable on many levels why a highly effective teacher is often selected to implement the treatment in the study. First, it is important to the integrity of the research itself that the treatment is carried out correctly and as close to perfect as possible. Typically, a highly effective teacher would be able to meet those demands much more than, for example, an ineffective teacher. If the treatment is not done to fidelity or its highest level then the researchers are really not testing the treatment and the study provides results that are inconclusive. If a study has low fidelity during the implementation of the treatment in the classroom(s) and the results of the study show that students do not make significantly higher gains than students who are in the control group receiving, for example, a study hall, one cannot automatically assume that this is true. After all, if you think about it, the treatment was never really studied. Therefore, it is understandable why studies that use classrooms and classroom teachers to implement the treatment select those teachers who have the ability to implement with high fidelity. However, this does pose a serious challenge to the generalizability of the study's findings to a wider audience. Generalizability of the findings does not pose a problem if the rest of the staff are as highly effective as the teachers who were used in the study. In many schools teachers possess a wide range of skills, experience, and effectiveness, and it is unlikely that a single school has a staff of all highly effective teachers. If this were the case, one could argue that these schools would not have a need for the intervention or program studied. Therefore, if a school was to adopt the treatment (shown to be effective in the study), it is most likely it would not experience the same level of impact, unless all the school's teachers were similar in their instructional level to the teachers in the study.

Process Implementation

School leaders and members of action research teams should closely examine experimental studies to determine *who* and *how* those administering the treatment were selected. If purposeful sampling was used (i.e., teachers were hand selected by principals and or researchers), then the characteristics used to select those teachers are critical to fully understanding the generalizability of the study's findings. For wider generalizability purposes, those administering the treatment should be randomly selected from a pool of applicants who represent a wide range of years of experience, background, and skill level. To address this, a researcher might have multiple teachers implementing the treatments and have these teachers present a wide range of backgrounds and skills. In this case, the researcher would want to include this information in the analysis of the study's data to determine if teachers with more of the desired criteria have students who make greater gains with the treatment than other teachers who possess less of these traits.

Emphasis on Professional Development

Did the study have to train teachers or other school staff to implement the independent variable (IV)?

How much training (or ongoing training) is required?

In addition to who is going to be delivering the treatment, it is also important for school leaders and action research team members to be aware of the amount of professional development that needs to occur. Professional development is not something that one instantly thinks about when examining experimental research, and although it might not necessarily impact the findings from a study directly, it does impact the generalizability of these findings. For example, it is highly probable that in order for the treatment (e.g., new reading program) to be implemented into the school, a certain amount of training needs to occur.

Quasi-experimental research is similar to experimental research except that it lacks one important characteristic: randomization. Although there are many quasi-experimental designs for researchers to choose from, these designs often contain a treatment and control group with pre and post testing done by the researcher for decades (Campbell & Stanley, 1963).

CAUSAL–COMPARATIVE RESEARCH

Another common type of research is **causal–comparative research**. Like experimental and quasi-experimental research, causal–comparative research also is intended to show a cause–effect relationship. Causal–comparative research is more similar to quasi-experimental designs in that it forfeits the use of randomization. However, it varies from quasi-experimental in that it does not use a pre–post design. In most causal–comparative studies, there is no opportunity for the researcher to give a pre measure before the independent variable (i.e., the treatment) is administered to the treatment group. In most cases, the treatment has already occurred and the researcher is coming in at the end of the study, presuming to know about everything that has transpired. The researcher examines the post data for the two groups and makes assumptions as to why the two groups fared differently on the post measure (Figure 6.5). If the individuals in the treatment group outperformed those in the comparison group (note that we didn't call this a control group since that is reserved for experimental and quasi-experimental studies), we attribute

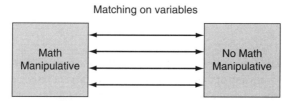

FIGURE 6.5 Causal–Comparative Research

that difference back to the treatment (i.e., the variable under study). This particular design, where one is at the end of the study and looking to the beginning to make cause–effect connections, is what is referred to as **ex post facto research** or after-the-fact research.

This particular type of research has been long called school principal research, since many times school administrators conduct this type of research in their school, unofficially as well as officially. For example, Principal Smith knows that Math Teacher A is teaching sixth-grade math and is using a lot of manipulatives. Every time Principal Smith passes by the class she sees students actively engaged with brightly colored blocks and chips and other types of manipulates spread out on their desks. She also notices that students are actively engaged and sees the teacher working through the problems that are being shown on one of the fancy new document cameras the school recently purchased over the summer. In another sixth-grade classroom down the hall, Math Teacher B is teaching mathematics using a more didactic approach. Teacher B is demonstrating how to solve a problem on the board, and students are following along and working through the problem on a worksheet. Students in this class appear to be well behaved and actively following the teacher's lead. At the end of the school year, Principal Smith examines sixth-graders' scores on the state annual mathematics assessment. She compares student performance (i.e., the post test) between Math Teacher A and Math Teacher B to see which class fared better on the state assessment. She finds that all but one student in Math Teacher A's classroom passed the assessment, and 10 out of 23 students failed the assessment in Math Teacher B's classroom. At the conclusion of her study Principal Smith relates the hands-on manipulates used in Math Teacher A's classroom to the increased student performance in relation to the lesser student performance in Math Teacher B's class. Take a minute to review this ex post facto study again. What are some other possible explanations for why students in Class A outperformed students in Class B on the mathematics assessments?

One possible explanation might be teacher variability—that Teacher A is a much more enthusiastic educator than Teacher B, and this is making more of an impact on student learning than the hands-on manipulatives. If you could do the study again, Teacher A would get the same results by working through problems on the board just like teacher B did. But Teacher A would be doing them with much more enthusiasm.

Another possible explanation that you may have thought of has nothing to do with the treatments but is due to the actual groups or classes of students. Could it be possible for Class A to be a different mixture of students than Class B, that Class A students love math and believe that they are good in math, although students in Class B are struggling mathematicians?

To do their best to address this, researchers conduct what is called **matching**. In the preceding example, a researcher would literally take a student in Class A and find a match in Class B. If the researcher cannot find a student to match, the researcher simply excludes this student's data. If by doing the matching, the researcher realizes that the students across the two classrooms are really not the same, then the researcher should find two classrooms that have students that match across settings.

Summary

Reviewing the literature is another key step that is essential for the action research team. The review of the literature provides the foundation for the program or intervention that is selected by the action research team to address the issue or problem that has been identified earlier through data analysis. Several components make up the review of literature on a topic or issue. Empirical research, reviews of literature, opinion pieces, and how-to/practitioner pieces can all be found when beginning to conduct a review. Using an action research team can be a beneficial model when reviewing the literature. Although the review of literature may seem daunting, using an action research team can be a beneficial approach, with each member of the team reading, reviewing, and reporting on a handful of studies and articles.

Cause–effect research is often the most interesting type of research to school administrators and leaders since it attempts to answer the question "What works?" Experimental, quasi-experimental, and causal–comparative research are types of research intended to establish cause–effect relationships using two groups: a treatment group and a control or comparison group. Experimental research distinguishes itself from the other two because it is the only research where participants are randomly selected from a population and randomly assigned to a treatment and control group. Quasi-experimental research contains some aspect of experimental research but is generally lacking in true randomization. Causal–comparative research occurs with already existing groups (one group receiving a treatment while the other does not). No randomization occurs in causal–comparative research, and the variables under study have already occurred.

Key Concepts

abstracts
causal–comparative research
Educational Resources Information Center (ERIC)
empirical research
experimental research
ex post facto research
hypothesis
literature
matching
PsycARTICLES
PsycINFO
quasi-experimental research
randomization

Discussion/Reflection Question

As a current or future school administrator or school leader, what do you value about cause–effect research, and what are some of your apprehensions when using it to implement effective programs and instruction in your school?

Activities

1. This chapter presents some key components for school administrators and leaders to be aware of when reading and critiquing an experimental study. Select an experimental study that investigates an instructional intervention or program. Prepare a critique of the article. Be sure to indicate where you might expect to find some challenges with generalizing the study's findings to your own school.

2. Find a causal–comparative study that investigates an intervention or program. Read and critique the study. Generate a list of possible extraneous variables that might be interfering with the results of the study.

CHAPTER 7

Critiquing and Applying Correlational and Survey Research

After reading this chapter you should be able to:

1. Understand the basic intent behind correlational research.
2. Understand the basic types of correlational research: bivariate, prediction, and multiple regression.
3. Interpret correlational coefficients in determining the strength, direction, and statistical significance of the relationships among variables.
4. Understand the various methods of random sampling commonly used in survey research.
5. Understand the importance of response rate in survey research and strategies that researchers can use to help improve low response rates.

Vignette 7.1
Correlational Research and the Action Research Team

After successfully reviewing the research on cause–effect, next the action research team at Metro Middle School examined correlational and survey research. As with the cause–effect research, more discussions about what constitutes rigorous correlational research commenced.

"I know correlational research examines relationships among variables," said Mr. Finch, "but many times researcher examine variables and the findings seem to have little relevance to me as a teacher."

"I know what you mean," said Miss James. "For example, one of the studies that I came across on student school behavior said that there was a positive relationship between student attendance and student behavior problems in school."

"What does that mean exactly?" asked Mrs. Jennings.

"That a student who has high numbers of absenteeism also has a higher number of behavior incidents in school," said Mr. Finch.

> "That makes sense," said Miss James. "But again, what does that say for classroom application. It doesn't tell me as a teacher what I can do to address this issue, it just tells me that the variables are related."
>
> "Yeah, tell me something that I didn't already know," said Mrs. Jennings.
>
> "I feel the same way about survey research," said Mr. Finch. "Survey research seems to send surveys out to different groups of people: teachers, parents, students, and school administrators. It gathers their opinions or perceptions on an issue. For example, this one gathers what teachers believe are some of the causes for student behavior problems and what they believe could be done to address these issues."
>
> "I saw that article, too," said Miss James. "It was interesting and I enjoyed reading about it, but at the end of the day I couldn't figure out what the point of the study was."
>
> "I know the study didn't come to a final conclusion and state what were the best ways to address student behavior in school. It just kind of gave a summary of what the teachers said overall."
>
> As she had before, school leader Mrs. Jackson took notes about the action research team's discussion. Again, it was plain to her that she was going to have to provide the team with additional reading and resources about the purpose of correlational and survey research, how to critique these two different types of research, and, most important, how one could take research methods and findings from these studies and apply them to one's own school-level action research projects.

CORRELATIONAL RESEARCH

In Chapter 6 we discussed experimental, quasi-experimental, and causal–comparative research. These types of research studies use two groups and other research designs to draw a connection between a variable that is manipulated and the results or outcomes of the process. The purpose of correlational research is to show whether a relationship exists between two variables. More specifically, correlational research examines the strength or degree of the relationship, as well as the direction of the relationship (i.e., positively or negatively correlated) between variables (Lodico, Spaulding, & Voegtle, 2010). There is no attempt to manipulate the variables through random assignment, as is the case with experimental research. In correlational research, each subject or participant must have two variables. These variables are statistically analyzed to determine their relationship across the entire sample.

CAUTION ABOUT DRAWING CAUSALITY

You do not have to read too far into correlational research before you come across experts cautioning those new to the field not to draw causality between two variables—even when those variables are highly correlated. For example, many school districts have focused a tremendous amount of energy and resources on improving student performance on standardized assessments. Let's add to the example that research has shown a strong correlation between students improving on state assessments and students having an increased connection to school (i.e., having a sense of belonging). If you examine this study more closely, it does not state that school connectedness is not causing the increase in student achievement; nor does it state the opposite: that students' increase in school connectedness increases their academic achievement.

The same case could be made with a correlational study that examines professional development for teachers and student achievement. Such a study could show a strong correlation between an increase in teacher participation in professional development and an increase in student performance on a high-stakes assessment. With the emphasis currently being placed on high-stakes assessment and school administrators' effectiveness, it is easy to see how one would naturally want to make a causal inference. "We worked hard to provide teachers with lots of high-quality professional development and student academic achievement was our payoff!" Right? Well, maybe not. This relationship is only correlational because of the lack of randomization of subjects into treatment and control groups. The design used in correlation does not require randomizations or manipulation of a variable and, therefore, does not allow causal inferences to be made based on the evidence that it produces.

THE CORRELATIONAL COEFFICIENT

Since correlational research focuses on relationships and not causality, it is important for school administrators and leaders to understand how to interpret and read correlational research correctly. When two variables are statistically correlated, the result is called a **correlational coefficient**. This result or output is expressed in a number falling somewhere between +1.00 and –1.00.

For example, the coefficient for an increase in professional development hours and an increase in student performance on a standardized assessment might be expressed as .84. In examining this coefficient further, this would be considered a very strong correlation. Coefficients from .84 or greater are considered very strong, from .65 to .84 are strong, from .35 to .64 are moderately strong, from .20 to .34 are slight and 0 to .19 are considered no relationship or weak (Lodico et al., 2010).

In addition to the relationship between professional development and student achievement being a strong relationship it would also be considered a positive relationship as well. The positive or negative sign that accompanies the coefficient lets the researcher know whether the relationship is one that is positive or negative (i.e., inverse). A positive relationship is one where when one variable increases the second variable also increases, as in the examples above. Both variables can also decrease and still qualify as a positive relationship; however, when one variable increases and the other decrease (or vice versa) this is referred to as a negative relationship. For example, as the number of office referrals for students decrease, student performance in the classroom increases.

It is important to realize that a negative relationship deals only with the direction of the relationship. It has nothing to do with the strength of the relationships. Remember a coefficient's strength has to do with how far away it is from zero; therefore, a coefficient of –.86 is a stronger relationship than a coefficient of +.80, and a correlational coefficient of +.86 and –.86 are equal in strength (but not in their direction).

TYPES OF CORRELATIONAL RESEARCH

Although it is not the purpose of this book to make you an expert in correlational research, as a school leader you and your action research team should have an idea as to the different types of correlational studies that you will encounter when reviewing the research literature. In addition to understanding their basic purpose you will also begin to get a sense of how you and your team might use such research in your own action research.

Bivariate Studies

Bivariate studies are common in educational research. For this particular type of study, the researcher identifies two variables for each subject and then calculates a correlational coefficient based on the pairs of scores for each individual in the data set. The previous example of correlating professional development and student achievement was an example of a bivariate study.

Prediction Studies

Prediction studies are also very popular in educational research. The purpose of these studies is to predict what is likely to occur in the future. As you can imagine, these studies are important in education because we often don't want to wait (or have the luxury of waiting) to see how student performance factors out in later grades. We need to know now how students will perform in the future so we can make the necessary corrections and provide support to ensure that students are successful.

Unlike bivariate studies, where two variables are correlated, in prediction studies the positioning of the variables (i.e., first variable and second variable) is critical to the study's design. The **predictor variable** is the first variable in a prediction study. Students' scores on a state standardized assessment would be an example of a predictor variable. The predictor variable is determined before the second variable, or criterion variable. In such studies, the **criterion variable** would be gathered at some later point in time. The criterion variable in this case could be student ability to graduate from high school on time.

With this example the researcher(s) would have to wait until graduation and then access student school records and files to determine if the students have been successful or not in graduation. In this case, the correlational coefficient would show the strength and direction of how successful a predictor (the score on the standardized assessment) was at predicting the criterion (success in graduating high school on time).

Multiple Regression

Multiple regression is the most popular and widely used analysis in educational research—and for good reason. **Multiple regression** is popular because it focuses on a realistic problem not addressed by bivariate or prediction studies: the need to analyze more than two variables at the same time. Multiple regression allows the researcher to simultaneously examine relationships across multiple variables. It also allows the researcher to examine the relationship between two variables after the influence of other variables has been removed. As an added perk, multiple regression provides the researcher with the opportunity to see how accurately a combination of variables predicts a criterion variable (Lodico, Spaulding, & Voegtle, 2010).

STATISTICAL SIGNIFICANCE

In addition to knowing the strength and direction of the correlation, researchers can also determine if the relationships among the variables is statistically significant. To do this, researchers look to p-values. Although **p-value** may sound like a difficult concept, it is really a threshold or standard that researchers have decided is acceptable when interpreting the results of a study and deeming them significant. Researchers typically set the significance level at .05 or .01. When the p-value is less than the significance level ($p < .05$ or $< .01$), the relationship is said to be statistically significant.

When many variables are being correlated, researchers will often display the results in a table that is often referred to a correlational matrix. A **correlational matrix** is a display of all the various correlational combinations possible with the variables that are being examined. Researchers will generally indicate which correlations are significant with an asterisk. Discussion of which variables are significant will also be found in the results section of the study and should correspond with the matrix.

USING CORRELATIONAL RESEARCH

Correlational research can be used in many ways to help school administrators and action research teams improve student performance and other related issues. One of the most significant contributions correlational research can make to school improvement is to provide school leaders with quantitative evidence about certain variables that are highly related, as well as those variables with little or no relationship.

School leaders will also want to consider applying what they have learned about prediction studies to their efforts for ongoing school improvement. In fact, predictive studies could be some of the most helpful studies for school leaders and action research team members to examine. If you recall, the previous example had researchers waiting to see if students graduated high school in order to determine the predictability of the predictor variable. You could apply this process to your own school to evaluate the accuracy of the current internal assessments your school or district is using to monitor and predict student progress and achievement. Most schools today use some type of assessment to monitor students quarterly. This measure is not a high-stakes assessment but, rather, one that is instituted by the district or school and whose data are used for internal purposes; however, it would be important to determine how accurate these internal assessments are for predicting the level of student performance on end-of-year state assessments. If such efforts reveal that quarterly district assessments are not highly predictive of a student's future score at the end of the year on the state assessment, then the action research team would want to reexamine these district measures in order to improve their ability as predictive tools to monitor student success.

CRITIQUING CORRELATIONAL RESEARCH

Although it is in your action research team's best interest to examine and use correlational research to assist with ongoing school improvement efforts. It is also important to keep the following criteria in mind when critiquing studies and interpreting their results: reliability and validity of measures, sample size, and the shotgun approach.

Reliability and Validity of Measures

As noted, earlier correlational research uses quantitative data and requires at least two quantitative variables for each subject. Quantitative data for correlational research can be gathered from a variety of sources. In educational research there is an abundance of quantitative variables that researchers can correlate on students; many of these variables or data points have already been collected and are found by opening student files. Data that have been pregathered by some source other than the researcher are called **archival data**. Although it is perfectly acceptable to use archival data (and many researchers do), it is important when critiquing a correlational study to have a sense of where such data came from and what measures were used to collect it.

The authors of the study should not only describe how the archival data were accessed but also report on the quality of the measure(s) used to collect the quantitative data in the first place. What was the name of the measure(s)? Are these measures standardized? Are the measures reliable and valid? And if so, have they reported what type of reliability and validity have been established for these measures?

If such information on the measures has not been sufficiently reported on by the author(s) of the study, the data that are being correlated may be comprised. Results from the study should be subject to increased scrutiny by you and your action research team members.

Sample Size

Although we are taught to believe that large sample sizes are a good thing, giving greater generalizability of the study's results to a wider audience, in correlational research a large sample size should raise a cautionary flag. Large sample sizes can make even a small relationship between two variables significant. Therefore, results from correlational studies using large samples (n = 1,000 or more) should be examined carefully.

Shotgun Approach

In many cases, educational researchers have access to databases from school districts. Although a wealth of information is contained in these databases, one should not begin examining variables to see which ones correlate. This is referred to as a shotgun approach. Results from studies that take this approach should be examined with caution since it is possible that a significant relationship among variables could be reported when, in fact, the relationship is due to chance because all of the analyses are being conducted with many variables being examined at one time.

SURVEY RESEARCH

At first glance survey research may not seem that important to you as a school administrator or leader; however, despite initial impressions, a large portion of education research is in fact a descriptive survey of some form or another. Survey research is a quantitative research methodology, whereby the researcher develops research questions and then very carefully designs a research survey. Data collected from the survey will ultimately answer (or at least attempt to answer) the research questions that the researcher has posed.

The Role of Survey Research

Although school administrators tend to focus more on cause–effect research (i.e., what works), survey research plays a vital role in education. Perhaps there is no better way to appreciate survey research than to first understand its purpose. The purpose of survey research is to gather people's perceptions and understanding about educational issues, processes, or products. For example, a survey study could survey new teachers entering the profession to find out what they (the teachers) see as the biggest challenges to whether or not they will return to the school or the profession next year. The purpose of this study is not to determine whether a particular retention program is more effective than some other method used to retain teachers; rather, it is intended to get a sense of what those challenges are and how they impact teacher turnover rate. For a school leader, knowing this level of information is very important. If we are able to better understand the why's, then we have a better chance of developing a program, a series of trainings, or better infrastructures and systems in our schools to address these issues.

Using Survey Research

The action research team should not exclude survey research from the literature that they review during their data analysis and program development process, as described in previous chapters. As with the preceding examples in this chapter concerning survey research with new teachers and teacher turnover rates, if the action research team were to come across such a study that identified key reasons for turnover rates, team members would want to consider using those data to help inform the program's characteristics for implementation in their school.

HOW TO CRITIQUE SURVEY RESEARCH

Population

Although there are many purposes for why one conducts survey research, ultimately survey research is conducted to gain a better understanding of what people think or do. In educational research, survey research often focuses on current topics or issues (e.g., what teachers think about high-stakes testing, or extra pay for increased student performance). Survey research is also used in education to understand how people do things or how these see a particular challenge with implementing a program (e.g., a new curriculum). Ideally, one of the main purposes of survey research is to identify commonalities across a large population. In research, a **population** is a group back to whom the researcher would ultimately like to generalize the results of the study. Survey researchers would ideally like to send a survey to the entire population; because of time, resources, and access, however, survey research uses random sampling to select a sample from the population with which to work. The sample is a mini-version of the population. The researcher prepares the survey and sends the final version to the sample. (Although we will explain random sampling, for now it is important to understand that random sampling is a process that allows a sample to be drawn from the population that looks similar to the larger population.)

Random Sampling Procedures

As noted, random sampling is a technique used by researchers to select a sample from a population. A random sample is done so that each individual in the population has an equal chance of being selected for the sample and an individual being selected does not interfere with another individual being selected. In its simplest form, a researcher can assign each individual in the population a number, starting at 1. Next, the researcher can select corresponding numbers out of a hat. Numbers selected from the hat correspond to the numbers assigned to the individuals, thus selecting them for the sample. Large studies, in which the population would number in the thousands or tens of thousands would use random sampling applications that are available in most computer software packages.

Stratified Random Sampling

In some cases, even though a researcher has carefully used random selection to draw a sample from the identified population, the sample does not look like the overall population. For example, let's say that the population was 50% male and 50% female; however, when the sample was randomly selected from the population, it is comprised of 80% male and only 20% female. If such proportions are essential to the study, then the researcher would want to use a technique to help ensure these proportions during the random sampling process. **Stratified random sampling** is a randomized sampling technique that helps maintain certain proportions between the population and sample. When conducting stratified random sampling, the researcher identifies the characteristics that need to be maintained in the sample. In the preceding example, gender would serve as that characteristic. Next, the researcher would determine the sample size and randomly select out half of the total sample size from the male portion of the population, and then repeat this process for the female portion in order to create a total sample that is the desired total sample size.

Cluster sampling is another random sampling technique that is often used in education research. Instead of randomly selecting individuals, in **cluster sampling** the research randomly selects entire groups in the sample to receive surveys. Although this random technique could certainly be used in other types of research, this approach is often used in survey research when the researcher does not have access to individualized information to use to send surveys. For example, randomly selecting school districts or individual schools from around the state and using those teachers within those settings might be more realistic (and timelier) than trying to obtain all names for individual teachers statewide.

Survey research that does not use a random sampling procedure but uses a sample that is readily available is referred to as a **sample of convenience or nonrandomized sample**. Action research team members should carefully examine the sample section of the survey study to determine whether the study sample used a random sample or a sample of convenience. Surprisingly, you will find that many survey studies use a nonrandomized sample. In many cases, this is done because of small populations. It is important to recognize that the finds from these studies are limited to the individuals in those settings.

Sample Size

When examining survey research, it is important for you and your action research team to make sure that the sample size is appropriate for the population from which it is drawn. A sample size that is too small when it is selected from a population could create a sample that is not representational of the entire population, and it becomes what is referred to as sampling error. Results from a sample that has been created through sampling error might be **homogenous**, or similar in nature, and therefore not generalizable back to the wider audience about which the study was originally intended.

Response Rates

In addition to sample size, you and your action research team should also carefully review the survey study to determine the response rate. **Response rate** is a term used by researchers to indicate the number of participants who actually returned the survey. In most survey studies the response rate is very different from the number of individuals who were sent the survey. Since not everyone who receives a survey responds, response rates are critical to interpreting and evaluating the results of the study, since many times people who are very pleased or very unhappy about an issue or topic tend to respond more readily to surveys than those individuals who are somewhere in the middle in regard to their beliefs on the topic. Low response rates in a study can, in turn, diminish the study's results. For example, if a study has less than a 50% response rate, it is impossible for the researcher (let alone the reader) to fully understand and report out what groups are thinking or believing. Let's say that a study has a 40% response rate, and for an item about high stakes testing 90% (of the 40%) of teachers respond that they are strongly opposed to high stakes testing. What does this really mean? Can the researcher make claims and say that the majority of teachers in the population are opposed to high-stakes testing? Can the researcher even make this claim in relation to the sample? The answer is no. Since the response rate is less than half of the participants originally found in the sample (those who received the survey), the researcher cannot attribute any results to the total number of participants found in the study. At best, the researcher could only attribute the results from those individuals who responded (i.e., the 40%) back to those specific individuals, since they most likely are very different from those in the sample.

In many survey research studies the response rates are even lower than 40%. It is not uncommon to see response rates of 20% or even 10%. It is important to keep in mind that these sample sizes are different from those discussed in the preceding example. In regard to sample size, it may be perfectly acceptable to have 10% of a population used for the sample, providing the population is large enough; however, this is not the case with response rates. Still, the action research team should be cautious when using findings from survey studies with very low response rates.

One method that researchers often use to address low response rates is to contact the sample participants again. The researchers do this by sending out the survey again or sending out a reminder notice. In the case of sending out reminder notices, if participants supply their name and the researcher is able to keep track of who has sent the surveys back and who has not, then the researcher only needs to send out reminders to those who have not returned the survey. In cases where the surveys are anonymous and even the researcher does not know who has returned the survey, then reminders have to go out to the entire sample. In cases where the researcher sends the survey to the entire sample again, it is important that the researcher clearly state to the participants that if they have already filled out the survey they should not do it again in order to avoid duplication. In a survey research study, the researcher should indicate the response rate, as well as steps that were conducted in order to improve or increase the final response rate for the study.

Sample Bias

Even if a survey research study has a large response rate, you and your action research team must also be aware of other elements that factor into interpreting the results. In order to conduct survey research one has to have access to the populations being studied. The ability to have access to populations plays a role in what is referred to as sampling bias. **Sampling bias** occurs when the researcher accesses a population and in doing so gets only a thin slice of that population (not a true representation of the entire population); sampling bias therefore severely limits the results to the population from which the original sample was drawn. In many cases, sampling bias occurs when the researcher is working with populations that are difficult to access. For example, let's say a researcher wants to survey homeless youth to find out where they live, what they do, how often they move, and what types of drug use they engage in on a regular basis. The researcher has been working with a not-for-profit agency that focuses on serving homeless youth in the city. The researcher gains access to the homeless population by surveying homeless youth over a month's time as they access the agency for medical services, food, clothing, shelter, and counseling. At the end of the month, the researcher has surveyed 99% of the homeless youth who actively engage with the agency for services. Sounds like the researcher did a good job, right? However, even though the researcher was able to access 99% of the population, results from this study are affected by the fact that not all homeless youth access services. Many homeless youth never seek refuge, food, or any kind of assistance. These homeless youth would therefore not be in the sample collected by the researcher. It is also possible that homeless youth who do not have access to or partake of services offered by this agency have substantially different traits, particularly when it comes to drug use. In fact, in reality the majority of the homeless youth population may not interface with any type of services.

In this situation, the researcher would want to develop other methods or strategies to get at the larger homeless youth population and not rely solely on access to this population through the agency. From this example you can begin to see the impact that sampling bias can play on both the interpretation and usefulness of a study's results. In cases where sampling bias cannot be adequately addressed, researchers should consider a different methodology or abandon the study altogether.

SURVEY DESIGN AND DEVELOPMENT

In addition to sampling, the researchers should also describe some of the processes associated with the design and development of the survey. In the procedure section of the study you and your action research team should determine whether the researchers piloted the surveys. When a researcher conducts a pilot of a survey, the researcher essentially field tests the survey. This is usually done with a small subgroup of the sample. This pilot group, as it is often referred to, not only participates in completing the survey but also provides written and/or oral feedback regarding the survey to the researchers. Often this feedback is provided in comments written directly on the survey and from focus groups. The purpose of the pilot is to improve the survey so that it collects the most valid data possible.

ADAPTING AND ADOPTING INSTRUMENTS FROM SURVEY STUDIES

Although you may not want to attribute those same results to your school and staff, you may want to consider using aspects of these surveys in your own school to collect data from teachers, staff, and related stakeholder groups. Even a survey study with a low response rate might prove to be beneficial in that the action research team can adapt and adopt all or portions of the survey instrument that was used in the previous study.

Copies of the surveys used in the study may be found in the appendix of the study. Because of pages limits, many journals that publish studies often do not publish the entire survey instrument. Most journals publish a section of the survey instrument or only examples of items. In helping you establish a better understanding of the instrument's design, be sure you and your action research team examine the instrument section of the research study. There the researcher should have explained in detail the various sections, items, and scales used to create the survey. If contact information is provided, you also might want to contact the researcher directly and inquire about obtaining a copy of the instrument for your own research in your school. Many times researchers are delighted to share their instruments with interested parties, so it is worth contacting the researchers with such a request. Starting with a template or basic survey will help you and your action research team in developing the best possible survey instrument so you can collect the essential data from staff while meeting your school improvement needs.

Summary

Correlational research differs from experimental research in that it does not manipulate the independent variable through randomization or any other research design. Because of this lack of manipulation, if a strong relationship exists between two variables it should not be considered causal. A correlational coefficient is used to determine the strength and direction of a relationship between two variables. Bivariate, predictive, and multiple regression are some types of correlational studies. In general, correlational research can be beneficial for those working on an action research team in that it allows team members to examine the relationship of variables, as well as a variable's ability to predict outcomes on a criterion variable. Such abilities would allow school personnel to determine the future success (or lack of success) of students while still allowing for time to address these matters with support and resources.

Survey research can also be an important component for members of the action research team. The purpose of survey research is to gather the perceptions of stakeholders about issues. In education these issues have a wide range, but many times the focus is on curriculum and instruction, high stakes assessment, parent involvement, and reasons for teacher and administrative turnover. Although many people may falsely believe that survey research is subjective and of little value, in actuality such findings can be invaluable in helping administrators and school leaders make critical decisions in their schools. Survey researchers can use a wide range of random sampling techniques in order to gather representative samples from the larger populations. These samples allow researchers to conduct their studies in more realistic terms with less time, resources, and organizational efforts. When critiquing survey research, action research team members should critically examine response rates as well as how researchers gained access to the populations and samples with which they were working.

Key Concepts

archival data
bivariate studies
cluster sampling
correlational coefficient
correlational matrix
criterion variable
homogenous
multiple regression
population
prediction studies
predictor variable
p-value
response rate
sample of convenience or
    nonrandomized sample
sampling bias
stratified random
    sampling

Discussion/Reflection Question

In this chapter you learned that even though there may be a very strong relationship between two variables, the relationship may not be causal. Keeping this in mind, what are some other possible explanations for student scores improving on a standardized assessment at the same time teachers are engaging in more professional development. (Remember, for those teachers who didn't participate in professional development, their students' scores went down.)

Activity

Select a current correlational and survey research study from the literature. Critique the study based on the criteria outlined in this chapter. Be prepared to present in class a short summary of the two studies and your critique.

CHAPTER 8

Critiquing and Applying Qualitative Research

After reading this chapter you should be able to:

1. Understand the purpose for qualitative research and the role and responsibilities of the qualitative researcher.
2. Understand some of the basic methods used by qualitative researchers to collect data.
3. Note several challenges with trying to collect valid data in the qualitative researcher process.
4. Understand some basic ways qualitative researchers try to improve the validity of their data.
5. Understand ways in which school administrators, leaders, and action research team members can use qualitative studies for ongoing school improvement.

QUALITATIVE RESEARCH

Qualitative research is different from quantitative research in that the researchers gather non-numerical data for the purposes of trying to better understand and explain how or why certain phenomena or processes exist in different settings. For many school administrators and leaders, qualitative research remains somewhat of a misunderstood mystery. One commonly held misperception is that qualitative data are not true data because they are not numbers. Not only is this belief completely unsupported, but it is also far from the truth.

Data are collected in qualitative research for a purpose different from that of experimental or correlational research. Qualitative research does not attempt to show that one variable is more effective than another or that one variable is inversely correlated with another. One of the unique characteristics of qualitative research is that it explains the commonplace and how things work. Although school administrators and educators often dismiss qualitative research, it might in fact be some of the most important information when working to improve practice and achievement in a school.

METHODS USED FOR QUALITATIVE RESEARCH

Qualitative research uses a wide variety of methods to collect data. Interviews and observations are perhaps the most common methods. When using interviews, researchers typically develop what is referred to as an **interview protocol**. The protocol usually consists of a series of open-ended items and works to guide the researcher through the interview process, as well as to standardize the interviews across different interviewees.

Conducting observations is another method used extensively by qualitative researchers to gather data. In such cases, researchers enter the settings (in education this would be schools and classrooms) and observe people working and learning in their naturalistic settings. Depending on what they are observing and the overall purpose of the study, researchers use an **observational protocol** or **checklist** to standardize their observations. Although they may vary, an observational protocol is a more open-ended data collection form. Both the observational protocol and checklist might have the researcher note general information (e.g., date, times, location, classroom level, number of students); however, a protocol would most likely not list specific things on which the researchers could focus. Instead, the protocol would provide a framework for the researchers to note their observations and write extensively on what they were seeing.

An observational checklist is a set of criteria for which the researcher is looking. Many times, researchers use checklists to count the frequency or number of times they observe a certain action or behavior (e.g., a student acting out or not on task during a lesson). Deciding on whether to use a protocol or checklist would depend on the study's overall purpose and the depth and breadth of the study's research questions.

Qualitative researchers also use archival data and records as part of their data collection process. Many of these archival records and data are quantitative in nature; however, they are still very much usable by qualitative researchers. In such a case, the qualitative researchers would most likely not conduct statistical analyses on these records (e.g., student raw scores on a standardized assessment) but would use them to cross-check or validate other data sources.

For example, let's say that qualitative researchers were following a small group of students who were receiving an intensive reading intervention designed to bring them up to grade level by the end of the school year. As part of the process, the researchers would interview and observe the students as well as interview the teachers, the school literacy specialist, and perhaps even talk to the students' parents or guardians. Then let's say that the data from all of these interviews revealed tentative findings that everyone (including the students) thought was an indication of great progress now that they are receiving the reading intervention. In this case, the researchers would also probably want to consult the students' records and take a closer look at the weekly reading assessments used to quantify the students' progress. Cross-validating qualitative findings with quantitative data is not only important but an essential element in good qualitative research.

ACCESS TO SUBJECTS AND SETTINGS

If you reexamine the different tools qualitative researchers use (e.g., observation, interviews, and document analysis), you will begin to recognize that these methods require the researchers to work in close proximity to the participants who are being studied. Although this is another unique characteristic that helps to distinguish qualitative research from quantitative, it does in fact pose some dilemmas. Working closely with participants allows the qualitative researcher to gather in-depth information that is so critically needed in good qualitative research; however, such "close quarters" can results in participants acting differently from how they "typically" perform or act.

For example, when a teacher is observed by his or her principal, the teacher reacts to the administrator's presence in the classroom. The teacher may try a little harder, move around the classroom a little more, or even have prepared more than usual the night before. Researchers refer to when one acts differently in the setting because of the researcher's presence as **observer effect**. Students are also affected by observer effect, and they too may act differently when the principal is in the room. In this case, the students may try a little harder, raise their hands a little more often, or act a little more interested than usual in the lesson.

Other than using a one-way mirror, observer effect is a reality for those qualitative researchers using observations. In order to control for observer effect, a qualitative researcher would use time. Dedicating a large amount of time to observations is perhaps the best way to diminish observer effect. In the case with the principal, if the principal observed the teacher every day for 2 weeks, the teacher and the students would begin to return to their typical classroom behavior. The teacher might not be so motivated or excited about the lesson and neither would the students. At this point qualitative researchers would want to start collecting their real observational data. Prior to this point, the researcher would be in the room observing and taking notes while recognizing that the data being collecting were not valid.

When the action research team is examining qualitative studies, it is important to pay particular attention to the amount of time the researchers were present in the settings they were studying. Too short of a time span (a few days here and there) could result in the researcher observing situations in which observer effect was occurring. Spending a month or so in the setting, for example, would allow researchers to observe the participants in their natural settings, acting as they typically do. The timeline for the observations would, of course, be dictated by the purpose of the qualitative study and the questions the researcher was pursuing.

Aside from observer effect the qualitative researcher has to control for observer bias. **Observer bias** occurs when the researcher brings to the setting outside biases that he or she has. For example, let's say that the researcher is biased because the school she is researching is in a "bad part of town" and therefore she believes the school is dysfunctional. Everything the researcher sees on entering the school is connected to the preexisting bias that she holds. Having such bias would certainly contaminate one's judgment in collecting and analyzing the qualitative data.

Qualitative researchers try to control for observer bias in many ways. In some cases, they keep a running list of their biases by writing down all their biases as they work through the research process.

Another technique used by qualitative researchers to control for biases is called member checks. **Member checks** is a process whereby the researcher sends interview transcripts and notes to participants for a cross-check validation (Lodico, Spaulding, & Voegtle, 2010). As part of this process, the researcher asks the participants to review the data and determine if the researcher has accurately portrayed the situation, the setting, and the participants' statements.

EXAMPLES OF QUALITATIVE RESEARCH

Although experimental approaches are focused on trying to show that an educational approach or variable is more effective than another, qualitative research focuses on trying to explain how. Here are some general examples of qualitative research:

- A study that investigates how one teacher is integrating portfolios into her fifth-grade ELA and mathematics classes
- A study that examines how parents of ESL students try to negotiate the school system when they themselves are non–English language speakers
- A study that examines how a parent involvement center was implemented in one school to increase parent involvement
- A study that examines how middle school teachers integrated LEGO robotics into their classroom
- A study that examines how a group of high school teachers integrated literacy across the curriculum using mini-technology projects and virtual field trips via the Internet

Although in some cases these descriptions may sound as though they could be quantitative (and possibly fall into experimental or causal–comparative research), the one aspect that sets them apart is that these studies are built around the process. These studies are all about capturing *how* people work and function in a particular setting and then providing an in-depth explanation of that process.

TYPES OF QUALITATIVE RESEARCH

Narrative Inquiry

If you like to tell stories (or listen to stories), narrative inquiry is a type of qualitative research that you will enjoy. In **narrative inquiry** the researcher collects stories about people's lives and experiences and then retells these stories along with interpretations and connections to a higher order of meaning. With origins in sociology and other related fields, narrative inquiry draws heavily on interviews as a main source of data, but also uses observations and documents to extend and support findings.

Case Studies

Case studies are perhaps the most popular type of qualitative research and can easily be found as the action research team begins to explore the research literature. One characteristic that separates this type of study from other qualitative studies is that case studies focus on a bounded system. A **bounded system** refers to a limited number of people who can be interviewed and/or observed for the purpose of the story. Let's take the preceding example about the students receiving a literacy intervention. In that case study, the researchers would most likely conduct interviews with the teacher, the literacy specialist, the students, and the parents. That would be the extent of who the researcher would want to interview—in other words, it is a bounded system.

Ethnographic Research

Unlike case studies that have a limited number of possible people from whom the researcher could collect data, ethnographic research has an endless possibility of participants. Using the same methods (e.g., interview, observation, document analysis), **ethnographic research** attempts to uncover themes and patterns about a large group or culture, as well as document the integrated complexities that exist within this setting. In the preceding case study the research focuses on the handful of students participating in the literacy intervention, whereas in ethnographic research the researcher would be interested in understanding an entire school district and community and the impact of ongoing lower student performance, high rates of illiteracy, and low student graduation rates. Because of the complexities that this research strives to document, it is common for ethnographic researchers to spend vast amounts of time in the communities and cultures that they are studying. In many cases, ethnographic researchers may move into those communities and reside for long periods of time in order to become one with the setting and culture they are studying.

Phenomenological Research

Phenomenological research could be called point-of-view research, attempting to see the world through the eyes of the participants. **Phenomenological research** examines people's interpretations of shared events or experiences and tries to draw patterns or connections to those understandings from the participants' perspective. Phenomenological research uses interviews as the primary method for collecting qualitative data, and although it may have characteristics that are similar to narrative inquiry or case studies, one key difference is that phenomenological researchers do not try to construct a sequenced story (i.e., a beginning, middle, and end) for the study.

USING QUALITATIVE RESEARCH

Despite some misperceptions about qualitative research, it is important for school administrators, leaders, and action research team members to understand the important role qualitative research can play in their efforts to improve their school. One of the most important contributions qualitative research can make toward school improvement is that it provides the school leader with perspective on an issue or phenomenon that he or she might never have had from this unique, in-depth perspective.

Since the purpose of qualitative research is to show processes and how they may work, it can provide action research team members with in-depth insight about certain phenomena and processes that they might not otherwise have been able to learn. For example, a qualitative study on new teacher turnover rate could be very informative to school leaders and administrators about the day-to-day issues that contribute to teacher turnover in schools. In addition, qualitative studies can provide school administrators and leaders conducting action research with some initial starting points for beginning to develop interview and observational protocols for the work they will be doing in their schools.

Summary

Although qualitative research may be overlooked by many school administrators and leaders, in reality it provides a very important component in working to improve a school. Qualitative research provides us with an appreciation and in-depth understanding of the commonplace as well as the multiple perspectives of the experiences and meaning made by others. Qualitative researchers use interviews and observations as their primary modes of data collection, along with examination of archival records, documents, and artifacts. Because of the close proximity to participants in the study, qualitative researchers have to ensure that the data they are collecting are valid and accurate. Controlling for observer effect and observer bias are examples of just two issues qualitative researchers have to be aware of when working in the field. Narrative inquiry, case studies, ethnographic and phenomenological research are a few different types of qualitative studies that exist in the research literature. School administrators and leaders working in action research should carefully examine qualitative research studies in order to gain a more in-depth perspective on the issue they are trying to address and insight into possible methods and questions they can use in their own school-level action research projects.

Key Concepts

bounded system
case studies
checklist
ethnographic research
interview protocol
member checks
narrative inquiry
observational protocol
observer bias
observer effect
phenomenological research

Discussion/Reflection Question

Take a particular issue in which you are interested. How would qualitative research methods be helpful in better understanding the issue from the perspective of the teachers, staff, parents, and students who work and learn in your school?

Activity

Select one of the studies from the following list. Review the study for both content and research methodology. What methods did the researcher use to make this qualitative research? Review and critique the study and be prepared to present a short 10-minute presentation to the class.

- Gigante, N. A., & Firestone, W. A. (2008). Administrative support and teacher leadership in schools implementing reform. *Journal of Educational Administration, 46*(3), 302–331.
- Hemsley, J. (2004). A partnership approach to using research: The role of the LEA. *Management in education, 18*(5), 17–20.
- Krueger, K. S. (2009). A case study of a rural Iowa school preparing to meet new state guidelines for school libraries. *School Library Research, 12*, 31.
- Meier, E. B. (2005). Situating technology professional development in urban schools. *Journal of Education Computing Research, 32*(4), 395–407.

CHAPTER 9

Gathering Data from Staff and Other Stakeholders

After you read this chapter you should be able to:

1. Understand why a school leader needs to gather staff and stakeholder perception data as a vital step in the school-level action research process.
2. Understand the basic components of designing and developing a survey.
3. Understand the basic parts of a survey and the appropriate scales to collect valid data.
4. Understand the key aspects of writing valid survey items.
5. Understand the most appropriate method for collecting valid survey data from staff and other stakeholder groups within the school.

Vignette 9.1
The Action Research Team and Gathering Additional Data

John Saxton is the school principal at Smithtown Middle School. He has been in the position for only 1 year, but in that time, he has managed to gain the respect of his teachers and support staff. According to one of his teachers, gaining this respect was not an easy feat, as teachers at Smithtown Middle School tend to be suspicious of administrators. "Mr. Saxton is a leader who does what he says he is going to do," explained one of his teachers. "He is someone who follows through with the initiatives he puts in place. Before he came, we had principal after principal. They came in, came up with a plan (usually on their own), and then left, never really getting anything off the ground. Mr. Saxton has always done what he says, and the staff here knows he won't let us down or disappoint us."

In addition to completing what he sets out to do, Principal Saxton also has addressed many issues in the school. The next issue that Principal Saxton needs to address is student behavior. As a participatory member of the action research team, Principal Saxton, along with four members from his teaching staff, has been examining student behavior data.

Based on their data analysis, they believe that they need to have a program that not only serves as an intervention, but also assists them in collecting more formative data. They also believe that a schoolwide program is necessary, particularly one that focuses on positive reinforcements and sets a particular philosophy or tone for the school.

In reading some of the research on schoolwide behavior plans, Principal Saxton and the school's action research team came across many research studies pertaining to using a framework called Positive Behavior Intervention System (PBIS). Overall, they found that the research on PBIS sounded very promising. Although they could find no experimental research on the subject, they did find program evaluations as well as some studies with comparison designs. These studies showed that schools that implemented PBIS programs had a notable decrease in the number of student behavior issues, office referrals, and in- and out-of-school suspensions. In addition, these studies reported that students made gains in other areas associated with behavior. These gains include respect, a sense of self, and a sense of community and school connectedness. In addition, the PBIS framework included a token system in which students received tokens for exhibiting targeted behaviors. These tokens were redeemable for prizes at the school store. The previous administration had implemented a school store, and even though not much was happening with it, everyone on the action research team (including Principal Saxton) saw it as a good way to revive a past initiative.

Knowing that he needed staff input and buy-in, Principal Saxton worked with the action research team to develop a staff feedback survey. In a short after-school meeting, the action research team put together some questions for the survey. They prepared to administer the survey at a mandatory information meeting that they were holding for teachers and staff about the behavioral issues in the school and the action research team's potential solution.

At the conclusion of the information session, the survey was disseminated to teachers. The teachers were instructed to fill out the survey before leaving. As they were completing their surveys, Principal Saxton took the opportunity to reassure his staff how important their feedback was in helping the action research team select an initiative. Principal Saxton then stood at the exit, personally thanking each teacher as he or she handed him the completed survey. Seeing that the principal was collecting everyone's survey at the door, several teachers began to change their answers. Someone from the teaching staff could even be heard asking, "Does anyone have a pencil with an eraser?"

Later that same day the action research team began to analyze the survey data. The action research team was pleased that all the teachers completed the survey. "A hundred percent," replied Principal Saxton at the action research team meeting the next day, "that's really impressive." From his reading on using surveys, he recalled that one of their challenges was getting a rigorous response rate. In some cases, research studies had a response rate of less than 30%; that would not be enough information to make any reasonable inferences.

As the action research team began to go through the data, they noticed that many of the teachers had skipped questions. In some cases, teachers had indicated a question mark beside several of the items asking them for their grade level, years of teaching in general, years at the school, years in the district, and so on. Many teachers wrote notes or explanations in the margins to try to explain their answers further. After reviewing all the teachers' surveys, Principal Saxton and members of the action research team reached an unfortunate conclusion: Even though the staff tried their best to fill out the survey, the survey was not well designed. They had achieved an impressive 100% return rate, but the data that they had gathered from staff were not usable. The data would not be useful in helping the action research team make a decision about how to move forward and address the student behavioral issues within the school. There was no way for Principal Saxton or members of the action research team to know what the staff's consensus was on the topic of behavior or the growing behavioral problems within the school.

Principal Saxton did not know what to do. How would he respond when staff asked him what the survey data had shown the action research team? What would he and the action research team write in their final report? What could he have done differently in designing the survey?

GATHERING FEEDBACK WITH THE SURVEY

Presented in Exhibit 9.1 is the survey developed by Principal Saxton and members of the school's action research team. Review the survey and note any problems that you see with its ability to collect valid or accurate data.

As demonstrated by Principal Saxton, the act of collecting feedback from staff is one of the key steps in school administrators conducting schoolwide action research. Although it did not go

| EXHIBIT 9.1 | Sample of Survey at Smithtown Middle School |

Staff Feedback Survey

School Safety

We are interested in gathering information from you for studying school safety and student behavior. Your responses are confidential and will not be shared with anyone outside of the action research team. Thank you for your time.

About you:

Your Role (please check one):

_____ Teacher _____ Special Education Teacher _____ Educational Assistant

_____ Secretary or Support Staff _____ Other: _____

How many years have you been teaching? (please check one)

_____ 1–3 _____ 3–6 _____ 6–8 _____ < 9

How many years teaching in this school (please check one)?

_____ 1–3 _____ 3–6 _____ 6–8 _____ < 9

Grade Level You Teach (please check one):

_____ 9th _____ 10th _____ 11th _____ 12th

Read each of the following questions and respond using the following scale:

1 = Strongly Disagree; 2 = Slightly Disagree; 3 = Neutral;
4 = Slightly Agree; 5 = Agree; 6 = Strongly Agree

1. I disagree that student behavior is not a major issue in our school.   1 2 3 4 5 6
2. Classroom instruction is often interrupted because of student behavior.   1 2 3 4 5 6
3. Problems start on the bus or in front of school and escalate throughout the day.   1 2 3 4 5 6
4. The cafeteria is a place where behavior issues begin.   1 2 3 4 5 6
5. Behavior problems often occur when students move from one activity to another within the classroom.   1 2 3 4 5 6
6. The school has well-established rules for students to follow.   1 2 3 4 5 6
7. All students, parents, teachers, and support staff are very well aware of the rules and their consequences for the school.   1 2 3 4 5 6
8. When students return from the cafeteria, I often have problems in the classroom.   1 2 3 4 5 6
9. The school has done a good job of informing parents what is expected in the way of students' behavior.   1 2 3 4 5 6
10. Don't you think we have a behavior problem here at Smithtown Middle School?   1 2 3 4 5 6
11. We really need a PBIS program here at the school.   1 2 3 4 5 6

particularly well for Principal Saxton, it is a critical component for several reasons. First, it provides the school administrator and the action research team with data to help guide the decision-making process. Second, it allows the school administrator the opportunity to show staff that they too have a role and a voice in what types of initiatives and programs are implemented in the school for overall school improvement. Third, it provides the school administrator with an opportunity to foster new and old relationships with staff and to work to build community. Too often, gathering feedback from staff or other vested stakeholder groups (e.g., parents, community members, and students) is overlooked during the planning and development stage of an action research project. If the school team goes ahead and selects an initiative or program without first gathering feedback from staff about the issue at hand (and their perceptions of how it can be fixed), the final plan will have little buy-in from the staff later on and could even be met with resistance.

WHY FEEDBACK IS NEEDED

It is important for school leaders to be able to read the pulse of their schools. Effective school leaders do not want to lose touch with the people in their schools. They need to know what staff members are thinking and feeling at all times. Research has shown that a common trait shared by highly effective school leaders is that they try to get a reading of their staff before making curriculum or other major decisions for their schools (Whitaker, 2003).

Depending on the issue that needs to be addressed, a school administrator may select different groups to gather perceptional data. Teachers and support staff would certainly be the first tier of stakeholders a school leader would want to gather feedback from concerning a possible action plan for school improvement; however, in some cases, parents, community members, and even students may be viable groups to gather data on an important issue.

METHODS FOR GATHERING FEEDBACK

There are several main methods for collecting feedback data from staff and other groups associated with the school community. In applied research, these methods are referred to as self-developed and come from both quantitative and qualitative research. Self-developed measures have to be created or designed by the actual researcher because of the uniqueness of the situation; already developed forms do not exist. In some cases, it may be possible to find a self-developed tool that is similar and modify it to meet your research needs.

THE SURVEY AND THE SCHOOL ADMINISTRATOR

A survey is a common method used by many school leaders to gather feedback from their staff and other vested stakeholders. A survey is a self-developed paper or electronic tool that gathers both quantitative and qualitative data from participants. Although it is a common method, most administrators have little, if any, specific training in how to design, develop, or administer a survey.

As demonstrated by Vignette 9.1, being successful in surveying one's staff is more than merely putting questions down on a piece of paper and handing it out to people. Developing an appropriate survey to gather the kinds of information that will help you as a school leader and the action research team make decisions is an art. Certainly, the more you use surveys, the better you will become at developing and administering valid ones. This section is designed to provide you with some useful techniques and ideas for developing surveys, as well as how to administer them to the respected stakeholder groups, to obtain accurate feedback from your staff, and to make sound decisions in guiding your practice and leadership.

EFFECTS OF A POORLY CONSTRUCTED STAFF SURVEY

In Vignette 9.1, Principal Saxton had staff willing to provide him feedback about the behavioral issues in the school and how successful they thought a PBIS system would be in addressing the problem? If he does not use that feedback, how enthusiastic do you think Principal Saxton's staff will be the next time he gives them a survey to fill out? How many times do you think a school administrator can collect data from staff and not use it before compromising his integrity? After all, Principal Saxton's staff may see things other than just a poorly executed survey. They could see it as a waste of their time. They also could see it as the administration not valuing their time as professionals, that the "so-called" behavioral problems in the school are trivial, or that the administration has already decided how it wants to deal with the issue and is going through the motions to make it look as though staff have a say in the matter. Unfortunately, because of past school history and a host of other reasons, many staff members may opt for the latter.

BASIC COMPONENTS OF A SURVEY

In order to build more rigorous surveys, it is important to understand the basic components or sections of a survey. Although these may vary considerably, some components should be found on a well-constructed survey: directions, demographics, and body.

DIRECTIONS. Although these will always vary depending on the issue being explored and the group the feedback data are being gathered from, **directions** are a key section for any survey. Without directions, individuals will not know what to do or how to answer the sections or understand the survey's purpose. If the directions are left up to the individual to figure out or assume, validity or accuracy of the data will be compromised. In addition, directions should be clear and well written.

DEMOGRAPHICS. **Demographics** are items on the survey that define or describe the individual who is completing the survey. Box 9.1 presents some examples of commonly used demographics.

BOX 9.1   Examples of Demographics

Common Demographics

Years of Teaching Experience _____

Grade Level __ 1st __ 2nd __ 3rd __ 4th __ 5th

School Type: __ Urban __ Suburban __ Rural

Current Position: __ General Education Teacher __ Special Education Teacher

__ School Administrator __ Technology Specialist __ Librarian

__ Teacher Aid __ Support Staff __ Other (please explain) _____

Although demographics may have nothing to do with the issue or problem you are gathering feedback on, they can be very important for analysis purposes. For example, a school administrator and action research team might want to look at the differences or similarities in teacher responses about an issue (e.g., student behavior). They may want to look for patterns in teacher responses on behavior based on the demographic item "Years of Teaching Experience." In doing so, they may want to see whether teachers who have been teaching for 10 or more years see the issue (or perhaps possible solutions) differently than, for example, teachers who have been teaching in the school for 5 years or less. If this is of interest, the action research team must decide on this early during development of their survey.

Before you put demographics on your surveys, it is important to realize that they might affect the quantity, as well as the quality, of the responses. Anonymous surveys contain little, if any, demographics. If the surveys are truly anonymous, you, the school administrator, cannot identify an individual who has responded. In Chapter 5, you learned about professional researchers conducting survey research and using anonymous surveys. The reasoning behind anonymous surveys is that respondents are made more comfortable, feeling that what they say cannot be tracked back to them. If respondents are more comfortable, they are more likely to tell the truth, as well as return the survey on time.

If you are planning to include demographics, you and your action research team might want to weigh the positives against the negatives before proceeding further. When working in small sample settings (i.e., a school district or school), anonymous surveys are highly recommended. Keep in mind even if you include only one demographic, such as grade level, in some situations it may be enough information to be able to track the survey back to an individual or even a small group of teachers. Even if that is not your intention, it may be the perception of those filling out the survey. If you want to create a survey that is truly anonymous, it is recommended not to use demographics for a sample of 99 or fewer. Keep in mind that this is not to say that you cannot use demographics; however, do not assume that the survey is anonymous in those small samples if you do choose to place demographic items on your survey.

BODY OF THE SURVEY. The **body of the survey** contains the items or questions that are being asked. In general, it is important to keep the length of your surveys short, particularly if you are using the survey to gather feedback from your staff. Your survey should be no longer than the front and back of a regular (8 × 10 or 11 × 14) sheet of paper. Any longer and it will impact the validity of the data as well as the number of surveys completed by your staff.

Since the body of the survey contains all the items, it also houses the scales. A **scale** coverts beliefs, thoughts, attitudes, or opinions (all of which are qualitative in nature) and converts them into quantitative data that can be analyzed using statistics. Likert scales, semantic differential scales, and checklists, are commonly used in survey measurement. Descriptions and examples of each follow.

Scales

Scales are wonderful because they help us measure constructs that otherwise would be difficult to quantify. Examples of these constructs would be people's beliefs, opinions, and attitudes about a particular issue or topic. The following are some examples of scales commonly used by professional researchers. They also can be helpful for school leaders and action research teams when developing a survey to collect perception data from staff and other possible stakeholder groups.

> **BOX 9.2 Alternative Likert Scales**
>
> **Frequency**
> Always, Very Frequently, Occasionally, Rarely, Very Rarely, Never
>
> **Importance**
> Very Important, Important, Moderately Important, Of Little Importance, Unimportant
>
> **Quality**
> Extremely Poor, Below Average, Average, Above Average, Excellent

LIKERT SCALE. Developed in 1930s, by Lenus Likert, the **Likert scale** is a common scale used in survey research. The Likert scale provides a statement to which one responds using a set scale. The traditional Likert scale was a 5-point agreement scale where 1 = Strongly approve, 2 = Approve, 3 = Undecided, 4 = Disapprove, and 5 = Strongly Disapprove (Likert, 1932).

The original Likert scale had a neutral response. Although in certain situations neutral can be an acceptable response, for decision-making purposes it is advised not to include a neutral option. For example, one of the mistakes Principal Saxton and the action research team made on the staff survey was that they included a neutral response. Of the teachers who reported, 80% were neutral on the issue. This type of feedback is difficult to decipher; however, if a scale had been used without a neutral response, it might have resulted in a finding such as 61% of teachers indicated that they were in slight agreement with the item. Not having a neutral opinion forces respondents to make a decision and lean one way or the other.

One of the attractions of using Likert scales is their amount of flexibility. Although the original scale was an agreement scale, alternative Likert scales allow you to measure different aspects. Box 9.2 presents a list of various scales that may be used.

SEMANTIC DIFFERENTIAL SCALE. Although similar to Likert scales, a **semantic differential scale** presents two opposite ideas (e.g., good and bad) and provides respondents with a scale. Box 9.3 presents some examples of semantic differential scales that you may want to use.

One of the benefits of using semantic differential scales is that you can ask respondents a series of different questions about the same topic, as illustrated in Box 9.4.

CHECKLIST. Another common scale used for surveys, the **checklist**, is not so much a scale as it is a list of items that respondents check off if applicable. Depending on the purpose of the

> **BOX 9.3 Example of Semantic Differential Scales**
>
> Good—Bad
> Cooperative—Uncooperative
> Serious—Humorous
> Boring—Fun
> Interesting—Uninteresting
> Important—Not Important

> **BOX 9.4 Integrating Technology into the Classroom**
>
> Interesting—Uninteresting
> Important—Not Important
> Needed—Not Needed
> Difficult—Easy
> Expensive—Inexpensive

checklist, respondents may be instructed to check off only one item, or in some cases as many items as they wish. One of the benefits of checklists is that they take relatively little time to complete. The limitation of checklists is that they typically do not gather process or detailed information. They do not tell the survey developer how something happened—just that it happened. Box 9.5 presents an example of a checklist.

OPEN-ENDED ITEMS. Another type of item is referred to as an open-ended item, or free response. **Open-ended items** require respondents to write their answers in detail. Open-ended items are good for gathering more in-depth information from respondents. For example, how do you go about working with the hands-on manipulatives when teaching multiplication of positive and negative numbers or how one goes about working with a difficult student. One of the disadvantages of open-ended items, however, is that respondents tend not to write as much detail as one would like. When someone answers an open-ended item with one or two words, it severely limits the amount of information a school administrator can use the data for in making a decision. In addition, too many open-ended items can discourage respondents from completing the survey. A school administrator should use caution when using open-ended items.

> **BOX 9.5 Example of a Checklist**
>
> Please check any foreseen challenges to implementing what you have learned at the technology workshop today.
>
> ___ Technical support
> ___ Time to practice
> ___ No or little access to equipment
> ___ School district firewalls
> ___ Money for further training
> ___ Focus on testing
> ___ Support from colleagues
> ___ Support from administration
> ___ Other: Please explain _____

TIPS FOR WRITING QUALITY ITEMS

Now that you have a better understanding of the different types of items that are available in survey development, you also should be aware of some basic elements for writing items in general.

Tip 1: Be Sure That Categories Do Not Overlap.

On surveys, we often create items that have categories for respondents to use. As shown in Box 9.6, these items are designed with the respondent in mind, taking only a second or two to complete; however, in creating items that have categories, it is important that the items be mutually exclusive and do not overlap. In Box 9.6, the item is asking respondents to indicate the number of years he or she has taught. By closely analyzing the categories, you can see where the problem lies. What would you check if you had been teaching for 3 years: the second category (1–3 years) or the third category (3–6 years)? Might you check both categories, or skip the question altogether? For validity purposes, it would actually be better if respondents skipped the item completely; however, respondents will feel compelled to respond and will generally pick the higher of the two choices. What if a respondent was in their first few months of teaching and had not completed a year? What would that person select? In an attempt to provide valid data, he or she would skip those items altogether; however, by checking "1 year," he or she would be rolled into the category with those teachers who have completed 1 year and are in the midst of their second year. If a school has a large proportion of teachers in their first year, this would skew the data and the results. Principal Saxton and the action research team could have addressed this issue by adding less than 1 year of teaching as a category.

Tip 2: Be Sure That You Use "Other" as a Response When Constructing a Checklist.

As previously noted, it is essential that you include the option "Other" along with the list of choices when posing a checklist. The reason that "Other" is so important is because it helps to keep the information the respondent is providing valid or accurate. Let's say that you survey community members who volunteer to mentor a high school student. As part of their responsibilities, the mentors take students to visit community colleges in the area. However, take a look at the survey item in Box 9.7.

As you can see, the checklist asks the mentors to "check off" all the activities they did with their mentee over the course of the school year. You also will notice that the creator of the item failed to include visiting colleges. If you were one of those mentors, how would you respond to this item? If you were going to respond in a valid manner you would skip this section and leave it blank; after all, you did not do any other things on the list. Respondents feel the need to check something off, however, and therefore some of the respondents may naturally search the list looking for items that are a close match to what it was they actually did. Let's say in this case that 80% of the mentors checked "Went to the library" because as part of the college tour they were shown the campus library and the facility and services available. As you can see, this is not an

---

BOX 9.6 Examples of Incorrect and Correct Categories

Incorrect: Number of Years Teaching? __ 0 __ 1–3 __ 3–6 __ 6–9 __ > 9

Correct: Number of Years Teaching? __ 0 __ 1–3 __ 4–6 __ 7–9 __ > 9

> **BOX 9.7 Another Example of a Checklist**
>
> **Check off all activities you did this school year with your mentee:**
>
> ___ Went to the library
> ___ Worked on homework
> ___ Discussed life in general
> ___ Talked about the future
> ___ Attended school games and events
> ___ Met with teachers
> ___ Participated in a community project

accurate depiction of what the mentors actually did for activities with their mentees. Not realizing this, the responses for that item are tallied by the survey developer, and a result that 80% of the mentors took their mentees to the library is reported.

Tip 3: Avoid "Neutral" When Using Data to Make a Decision.

As noted, if you are using the data for decision-making purposes (and as a school leader you are) it is best to avoid using a neutral choice. At the end of the day, it is best to know that your staff is leaning a little more toward "Slightly agree" concerning an issue than being neutral.

Tip 4: Avoid Double Negatives in Items.

You can see why it is important to avoid using double negatives with item 1 on the survey in Exhibit 9.1. If it takes a second or two to complete the "conversion" mentally before answering the question, many people might not take the extra time to think about the item before answering. The results are invalid responses that are on the opposite side of the scale from what respondents actually believe.

Tip 5: Only Measure One Concept at a Time.

This is well demonstrated in item 7 of Exhibit 9.1, where the question is trying to measure just about everything. What if a respondent marked "Strongly agree?" for this statement in regard to Teachers, but believed totally the opposite ("Strongly disagree") for parents and was somewhere in the middle for support staff? How would they go about accurately conveying this information? In a best-case scenario, they should skip the question altogether. Not answering is better than answering and having one's responses distorted because of poor item development.

Tip 6: Make Sure the Scale Is Accurate.

Make sure that all the scales in your survey match the choices presented to participants. In the case with Principal Saxton, one of the many challenges in obtaining feedback from staff with the survey (see Exhibit 9.1) was that the scale did not correspond to the options provided. After all, how would the action research team in this situation interpret participants who responded with a 5 on items. Such a mistake would make all data from surveys invalid because one would never know what people meant by a response of 5?

The order of the scale, such as 1 = Strongly Disagree and 6 = Strongly Agree, also is something that you should consider. Although there are differences of option as to how the scale should go (e.g., 1 = Strongly Agree and 6 = Strongly Disagree), it is recommended that you make the lower number associated with Disagree and the higher number aligned with Agree.

Tip 7: Avoid Leading Questions and Yes/No Responses.

Item 10 (see Exhibit 9.1) not only is leading, but if you examine it closely again it is impossible to answer using a six-point Likert scale because the response requires a yes/no response. Remember, Likert-based items are statements, not questions, so avoid starting items with the word "Do."

Tip 8: Spell Out Acronyms and Highlight Key Words.

There are several things wrong with item 11 (see Exhibit 9.1). Not only is it leading and requiring a yes/no response, but the term *PBIS* has not been defined for the respondent. Clearly defining the term will make it clear to the respondent what is being asked and will increase the validity of the data. When respondents have to guess what is meant by a term or answer an item with their own perception of what a term means, data and findings are distorted. An administrator could move forward on implementing a program or schoolwide intervention based on recommendations from her teaching staff, only to find that the teachers had a collectively different idea of what the program entailed, at which point it would be clear that the program in place does not resemble what teachers thought they were endorsing.

ADMINISTERING AND COLLECTING THE SURVEY

Now that you have developed a rigorous survey, it is time to administer it to your staff or the stakeholder group from whom you are interested in collecting data. Even though you have created items that will gather valid data, the method that you use to collect the data also will play a vital role in that data being valid or accurate. Surveys are not new to action research; in fact, they have been used extensively in applied research to gather the perceptions, opinions, and beliefs about a particular issue from a sample randomly selected from a population. In most cases, the action research team would not be gathering a random sample from the school population but, rather, from what is referred to as a census population. In a census sample, everyone in a stakeholder group would receive a copy of the survey. Census samples are usually more appropriate when the population of a particular stakeholder group is small in size (e.g., less than 200 individuals).

Now that the action research team has developed the survey, methods to administer the survey need to be examined. As illustrated in Vignette 9.1, how a school administrator and/or action research team administer and collect that survey has a great impact on the validity of the collected data. Table 9.1 presents the different methods one can use to administer a survey, along with their benefits and challenges.

METHODS FOR ADMINISTERING SURVEYS

As a school leader, it is important that you are aware that your role and involvement in collecting data from your staff have a great impact on the data's validity or accuracy (see Table 9.1). It is also important for administrators to be aware of the benefits and limitations for each method so that they can select the most appropriate method.

MAIL-OUT, MAIL-BACK (SASE). This method of survey dissemination continues to be the most widely used today. For this method, surveys are mailed out to participants. Along with a copy of the survey, each mailing contains a self-addressed stamped envelope (SASE) for the

Table 9.1 Overview of Survey Collection Methods and Impact on Validity of Data

Type of Data Collection Effort	Description	Implications for Validity of Data Being Collected
Mail-Out, mail-back (SASE); could include e-surveys	Mailed to school staff or stakeholders to address outside of school	Higher validity of data, low response rates
Hand-out, mail-back	Face-to-face administering of survey, but respondents able to mail it back on their own convenience	High validity of data, mailing addresses not required, can have low response rates
Hand-out and collect on site	Workshop style, collecting from participants after a session or training	Lower validity because of the close proximity between respondents and those responsible for collecting the data; however, high return rates
Hand-out on site, collect in drop box	Popular method used in school today	Higher validity providing more time for respondents and higher response rates if box placed conveniently in building where everyone has easy access; should not be placed in principal's office; however, action team must ensure confidentiality of data being collected and guarantee the security of the drop box.
Mail to site with point person to administer and collect	Often used with districtwide survey initiatives	Difficult to guarantee validity of the data; point person could tamper with data; this method should be avoided or conducted with a completely external impartial individual collecting data from across the various sites.

survey's safe return. This method is traditionally used by professional researchers conducting survey research, and it probably has remained so popular because of the unique elements this approach provides the participants. One of the unique benefits that the mail-out, mail-back method employs is that it provides participants the opportunity to read the items and fill out the survey in privacy. Whether the surveys are mailed to their home or to their place of work, the individuals who developed the survey (e.g., the administrator or action research team members) are not present or in close proximity to those individuals completing the survey. Having the survey developers elsewhere when the survey is being filled out should help to increase the validity or accuracy of the respondents' answers. In addition, if the survey is anonymous, the responses are likely to be even more valid. Anonymous surveys contain no demographic or other information that would allow the administrator or members of the action research team to know who filled out the survey. Research on survey development shows that people responding to a survey are more likely to respond truthfully when a survey is anonymous and the respondent feels that his or her responses cannot be attributed back to him or her in any way.

Although increasing the validity of the data is certainly important, the mail-out, mail-back approach does have limitations. One of the biggest challenges to this survey administration approach is that response rates are often considerably low. In survey research, a response rate is usually depicted as a percentage and can be calculated using the following formula: the number of surveys mailed out divided by the number of surveys that were completed and returned times 100.

One of the primary reasons that a school administrator or action research team would create a survey is to get feedback on how staff or some other stakeholder groups feels. Getting a low response rate would severely impact the ability to make such a decision.

For example, let's say that the school administrator sent a short survey to staff about the behavioral issues in the school and how, as a school, the staff might put a plan in place to address these issues. If the administrator sent out 100 surveys to staff members and only received 30 back (a 30% response rate), what type of assumptions can the administrator make regarding how staff feel about the issue? If your answer is "Not much," then you are thinking the right way. The fact that the administrator did not receive back a majority of the surveys (51%) makes it difficult to use the feedback data for any data-based decision-making purposes. In this situation, the administrator and action research team might make some conclusions as to the lack of responses from the staff. If you were that administrator, what might you conclude as some possible reasons for your staff's low response rate? The following is a list of possible explanations:

- My staff is very busy.
- Not a good time of year—state test next week.
- My staff is not interested in the issue.
- My staff doesn't think that this is a problem.
- My staff is one of status quo.
- The survey that I developed did not look inviting. It looked confusing or difficult and that it would take a lot of time to complete.

How many of these possible conclusions did you come up with? Did you think of the last one—that the survey was off-putting? In many cases, the way the survey looks, how it is constructed, how scales are used, and how items are constructed play a major role in the response rate. Even people who are very interested in the topic will quickly discard a survey that looks too long and cumbersome.

Another limitation for the mail-out, mail-back approach is the amount of time it takes to gather the data. As a general rule, surveys that are mailed back should have a deadline prominently displayed so that those filling out the survey are aware of the importance of their data.

How long should one give respondents to complete a survey? Naturally, the proximity of the survey developer to the respondent will play a role in the amount of time typically needed. In cases where the respondent knows the survey developer (such as the boss or the school administrator), 1 to 2 weeks is appropriate. In other cases, where it might be a researcher who has never met the respondents, 3 to 4 weeks may be more feasible. After that amount of time, respondents are less likely to complete and return the survey.

You can see that the time lag on mail-out, mail-back could be an issue for you as a school administrator needing to make a decision on how to address a particular issue or problem. In addition, you could wait several weeks to gather the feedback from your staff and then be faced with low response rates. If time is of the essence, then it is strongly recommended that you do not employ a survey administration method that requires respondents to mail back the survey.

HAND-OUT, MAIL-BACK. The **hand-out, mail-back** method is commonly used by school administrators to collect data from their staff or vested stakeholders. Although this method does require the respondents to mail back the survey, on the front end of the process an individual hands the respondent a survey. Although it may not seem like much, the face-to-face exchange between the survey developer and potential respondent can provide enough of a context to help slightly increase the response rates and response times. Think about when someone you know hands you something, and as they are handing it to you, they explain the importance of it, how they need the data back, and how the data are going to be used. They also have the opportunity to answer any immediate questions you, the participant, may have.

HAND-OUT AND COLLECT ON SITE. The **hand-out and collect on site** approach also is referred to as the workshop model, which is appropriate since it is commonly used in workshop settings. In this approach, the school administrator or members of the action research team hand out surveys personally to individuals who are gathered at an event, meeting, or activity. At the end of this meeting, respondents are asked to fill out their survey and personally hand them in before they leave. One of the advantages to this method is that in most cases the survey developers are able to collect all the surveys (100% response rate!). The only way that the developers would miss collecting a survey is if someone were sick absent, or not at the meeting. Another benefit of this approach is the immediacy in which the data are collected. If a decision needs to be made, then this approach is your best choice for collecting data swiftly.

Despite the benefits of this method, two serious limitations are worthy of consideration. The first limitation has to do with the time you give respondents to reflect and think about the issues. Because you are collecting the surveys on site and giving respondents, for example, 10 to 15 minutes to complete them, you may be rushing them through the survey. If this is the case, respondents might make mistakes, not read closely, and select first ("gut") feelings for responses. All of these possibilities will impact the validity or accuracy of your data.

The second limitation to think about is your presence on the site. The fact that you, the school administrator, are collecting the surveys on site as they are handing them to you may dramatically impact the responses of your staff or stakeholders. In other words, since you are in the power position, staff might change or modify their responses to be more politically correct or socially acceptable since they know you are collecting the surveys on the spot and might be able to connect their responses directly to them. This is what happened in Vignette 9.1 at the beginning of this chapter. When the staff realized that their principal was collecting the surveys at the door, they became restless and started altering their responses to the questions on the survey.

HAND-OUT ON SITE, COLLECT IN DROP BOX. A popular method used to collect data in schools is the **hand-out on site, collect in drop box**, or drop-box, method. This employs the use of a lock box located somewhere outside the principal's office where staff and others can drop off their surveys when they have completed them after a meeting. One of the benefits of this approach is that it gives staff ample time to gather their thoughts and respond to the items accordingly. This way, staff will feel more comfortable that their responses will be mixed in with those of others; thus they are more likely to provide valid, honest answers. Although this approach is used often, it is important for administrators to realize that they are ultimately responsible for securing the drop box and protecting the confidentiality of all those individuals who filled out the survey.

MAIL TO SITE WITH POINT PERSON TO ADMINISTER. This method, **mail to site with point person to administer**, is not one that is recommended, although it is often used in school settings to gather perceptional data from staff for district and state-level purposes. Let's say, for example, that the district is surveying teachers, staff, or students across six different schools. Surveys are bundled into a large envelope and sent over to each school. A point person, in many cases the principal, is designated to disperse and then collect the surveys from staff and mail them back to the central office. Although this may be an efficient method for collecting mass surveys across the district, it has many potential flaws. The main limitation is that the point person could take liberties in handing out the surveys: Handing surveys out to teachers that support the point person's opinion or agenda, or sorting through completed surveys and discarding those that do not, could paint a favorable picture. One way to control for this is to record the number of surveys that are sent to each school. For example, School A has 100 teachers; however, only 40 surveys are returned. This low number could be because of tampering with the surveys or the natural low response rate. It is difficult, if not impossible, to differentiate between the two. Another way to help prevent tampering is to number surveys, such as 1 out of 100, 2 out of 100, and so on, to let the point person know that the surveys are being tracked.

Summary

Developing a survey takes a lot of time, expertise, and knowledge. If done correctly, a survey used to gather data from school staff and other vested stakeholder groups can be invaluable to the action research process—giving the action research team yet another set of data to work with in step 1. If the survey, however, is not well designed or well orchestrated, the results can be disastrous and can undermine in many ways the good work that an administrator or school leader has done to foster relationships with staff and the school community. In addition to writing clear, concise items to collect valid data, the action research team also must ensure how they collect the data from school staff so that their actions do not interfere with the survey's overall validity. It is important that the action research team consider the issue that is being addressed when determining the method used to administer and collect data from school staff or other identified stakeholder groups.

Key Concepts

- body of the Survey
- checklist
- demographics
- directions
- hand-out on site, collect in drop box
- hand-out, and collect on-site
- hand-out, mail-back
- Likert scale
- mail to site with point person to administer
- mail-out, mail-back (SASE)
- open-ended items scale
- semantic differential scale

Discussion/Reflection Questions

1. If Principal Saxton and members of the action research team had the opportunity to do the survey again, what changes should they have made to it? Are any of these changes different from the initial list that you made before you read this chapter?
2. List key things this chapter has taught you about gathering feedback data from your staff. What learning points will you bring back and use in your professional practice?
3. At the end of the vignette, Principal Saxton and members of the action research team are faced with a serious dilemma. Let's say that they decide that they cannot use the data in their report to staff. Knowing the legacy of the past administration, should Principal Saxton tell his staff?
4. What approach did Principal Saxton take in administering and collecting the survey? Was this the best approach? What are the benefits and limitations that may help or hinder the situation?

Activity

1. Pretend that you are a principal in a school similar to Smithtown Middle School. Like Principal Saxton, your school also has a problem with student behavior. Recreate the survey in Exhibit 9.1. Then project the kinds of findings you would have if you administered it to your staff and how that data would help guide you in selecting and implementing a practice to address the issue at hand.

CHAPTER 10

Step 2: Developing a Program for School Improvement

After reading this chapter you should be able to:

1. Understand and define what a program is.
2. Define what a logic model is and its main components.
3. Describe how logic models work and how change theory is presented.
4. Discuss why a logic model is better suited than a traditional experimental design to show cause–effect relationships for many action research projects.
5. Understand how you, as a school leader, can use a logic model when working with your staff and action research team.

Vignette 10.1
The Action Research Team and Implementing a Program

Principal Johnson has been the principal of Bryant Middle School for 3 years. When Principal Johnson took the position students across all three grades (sixth, seventh, and eighty) were not performing well on the state's annual English language arts (ELA) assessment. Working collaboratively with his action research team, Principal Johnson decided to focus on technology, believing that through teachers integrating technology into the classroom (e.g., blogs, webinars, virtual field trips, Web publishing) students would improve their writing and thus improve their performance on the state's annual ELA assessment.

Two years ago, recognizing the need to improve student performance on the ELA assessment, Principal Johnson and his action research team focused on integrating technology into every classroom in the middle school. Through a state grant, new computers were purchased and installed in the building. In addition, the building's Internet capacity was greatly improved. Teachers received a series of professional development sessions on how to use technology and how to integrate technology into their classrooms to increase students' writing. Although the professional development sessions (i.e., activities) were well done, they did not deal with the more sensitive issues surrounding teachers integrating technology into their classrooms.

Although teachers were interested in blogging and webinars, they were also scared that they would somehow "break" the equipment or "mess up the Internet," and they didn't want the school to spend more money fixing their mistakes. So although they had access to the equipment and resources to conduct virtual field trips and videoconferences, the teachers did not use the equipment or create blogs or Web sites to increase the amount of writing and collaboration of students.

At the end of the school year student performance improved on the state's ELA assessment. Inspired by the results, Principal Johnson implemented another series of professional development trainings on even more advanced technologies that teachers could use in their classrooms. Following the second year of technology trainings, students did not perform as well on the state ELA assessment. In fact, scores dropped considerably and Principal Johnson decided to drop the technology integration program altogether and focus on using a new literacy curriculum for the school. Two years later when the new literacy program did not improve ELA scores, Principal Johnson decided to implement yet another literacy program. This new program also proved to be unsuccessful in improving student performance. Soon after, Principal Johnson left Bryant Middle School to take another position in another district.

DEVELOPING QUALITY PROGRAMS AND INITIATIVES

After completing all the components of Step 1, it is time for the action research team to move to Step 2: Developing a Program (see Figure 10.1). In an ideal world a big book would be filled with detailed descriptions of foolproof programs. In an even better world this book would have chapters organized into solutions for solving schools' biggest problems. In the best world possible these issues, once addressed, would stay fixed for school administrators to work on other issues on the pathway to school improvement. Unfortunately, there is no such book; however, as noted in previous chapters, we do have a wealth of knowledge and research supporting educational practices and programs. And although consulting the literature and research on how to address an issue in your school is recommended, unfortunately reviewing the literature and past research is not enough. Effective school leaders need to take research-based practices and interventions, implement them into their school, and then conduct their own school-level studies of those programs in order to fine-tune them for their school.

ALIGNING NEED TO PROGRAM ACTIVITIES

A program is a series or set of related activities that are temporarily conducted to address a specific issue or problem. (At the end of any action research project, the ultimate questions that everyone wants to know is this: Was the program or initiative a success? In other words, was the

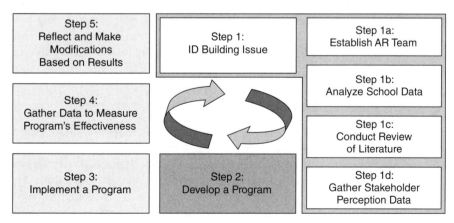

FIGURE 10.1 Steps in School Level Action Research Process

action research project able to address the issue or problem in the school? All in all it seems as though this is a logical question to ask and an even simpler one to answer, right? "Yes, it worked" or "No, it didn't."

As you learned in Chapter 3, ideally the best research method for answering this question (Was the program or intervention effective?) would be to use an experimental or quasi-experimental design. If you recall, this design randomly assigns participants to treatment and control groups and works to control for extraneous variables. The purpose of these designs is to be able to infer causality back to the treatment or independent variable if participant performance in the treatment group is significantly different from that of those in the control group. However, as previously noted, only in rare circumstances does one have the opportunity to conduct experimental or quasi-experimental research in a real school setting. Parent or guardian permission forms, appropriate settings, and school class schedules are only a few of the logistical and ethical challenges inherent in trying to implement such a research design in a school. Because of these challenges, it is unlikely that you or your action research team will be able to answer this question through an experimental or quasi-experimental design. This type of research is best left up to the professional researchers conducting applied research.

In Chapter 1 you may recall reading about how school administrators and leaders have tried to link the activities they have implemented into their school (e.g., technology, new reading and math programs, professional development) with changes on various outcomes measures (e.g., state assessments in ELA and mathematics). We refer to this as gap analysis. Figure 10.1 is an example of this process. This is where school administrators and teams have analyzed data, identified gaps in the data that need to be addressed (e.g., an overrepresentation of males in special education or a large gap in the performance of English Language Learner (ELL) students with the general education population in the school) and have implemented measures to address these issues. In order to determine whether or not their efforts have been successful, school administrators and teams examine the final outcomes (e.g., change in test scores) and attribute any change to their initial effort.

INTRODUCTION OF THE LOGIC MODELS

Frustrated by many of the same limitations in determining what works, professional program evaluators who examine and determine the "worth" or effectiveness of programs began to use what is commonly referred to as a **logic model**. As you can see in Figure 10.2, logic models are graphic organizers or flowcharts. Their purpose is to show connections within and among the various parts of a program or initiative (Fretchling, 2007) and pinpoint precisely how a program's activities support the theory of change. Take a moment to examine the logic model in Figure 10.2. Based on what the logic model shows, can you figure out the overall purpose or goals of this program?

WHY USE A LOGIC MODEL?

Up to this point, the logic model has been described as a tool for showing how programs and interventions will achieve their goals or outcomes (e.g., create change). You may find that discussing a logic model seems a bit odd right now, especially since this chapter is supposed to be about developing and designing quality programs and interventions. Although this may seem to be the case, the answer is that in reality the logic model can be used to accomplish both tasks: to provide the linkages between activities and outcomes as well as to serve as a framework for developing quality and purposeful activities.

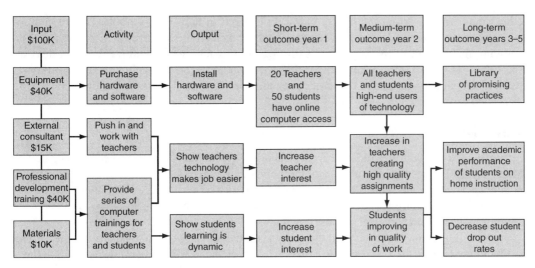

FIGURE 10.2 Example of a Logic Model

LOGIC MODEL: BASIC BUILDING BLOCKS

To better understand what a logic model is, one must first have a fundamental understanding as to the basic parts that make up these models (see Figure 10.3).

You can see inputs, activities, outputs, and outcomes in this basic logic model. Essentially, the purpose of the logic model is to lay out the relationship between activities and outcomes within a program before the program is implemented. In an effort to predict what these relationships are before they occur, the logic model helps to establish that the program did indeed result in the outcomes that were observed.

Inputs

Inputs are generally the first component of most logic models. According to Fretchling (2007), inputs are resources, monetary funds, and in-kind contributions that make such efforts or new initiatives possible. In some cases, inputs would also be a group's mission or a new vision that the school or district is now charged with completing. Although it may appear to be an activity, the gap that is identified through analyzing data could also be perceived as an input, since activities will now have to be created in order to address the gap. An evaluation report by the state department, district, or direct supervisor could also be seen as an input. Such reports clearly identify areas that need to be addressed or improved on within a school.

Although it may not seem necessary, it is important to fully describe the inputs in the logic model. As noted by Frechtling (2007), accurately noting all the various resources to more fully describe the inputs is important for many reasons. The main reason for describing all the inputs is for purposes of replication. If at the end of your program results are favorable,

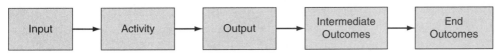

FIGURE 10.3 Basic Components of a Logic Model

others may want to adopt the program and replicate it in their own schools. Having a complete picture of the resources that were necessary to launch this effort is critical. In addition, knowing the amount of resources that were required to achieve the end result might also assist others in determining whether they have the capacity to even begin such an initiative, particularly since many times resources play a critical role in the successful implementation of certain programs.

Activities

Activities are the building blocks for any school-level action research project. According to Mathison (2002), a program is a series of temporary activities designed to make an improvement or address an identified issue. Programs are made up of a series of related activities working together to achieve a collective purpose or goal. For action research, these programs could be wide ranging in their characteristics, purposes, and goals.

You might now be wondering how many activities should constitute a program. According to Frechtling (2007), this is a common question asked by many who are working with logic models for the very first time. Although it is impossible to set an exact number for into how many activities a program should be divided, it is important not to break the activities into too fine a grain (Frechtling). Getting too specific about a program's activities can bog down a logic model, making it too clumsy or awkward to use effectively. However, quite the opposite is true, and by not breaking down the components on the logic model enough, you are left with a model that is too broad and too general for any meaningful discussion for your action research team. Again, although it is impossible to say for certain how many activities are appropriate for a logic model, for most, five to eight main activities are deemed appropriate. As you and your action research team work more with logic models you will become increasingly more comfortable with them and begin to develop a feel for determining the grain necessary for projects based on their purposes, goals, and potential outcomes.

For example, let's say that your action research team decides to implement an after-school program to provide enrichment as well as tutoring and academic services for students. Under the activities section of the logic model, you and your action research team would want to think about the various activities that would make up the entire program. Again, you and the action research team would want to divide the program into core activities. **Core activities** are the main activities that occur on a daily or regular basis. Presented in Figure 10.4 is a breakdown of what

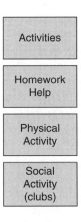

FIGURE 10.4 Example of Activities

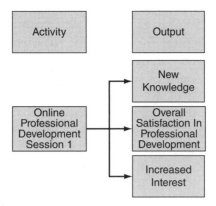

FIGURE 10.5 Example of Outputs from Online PD

an action research team determined to be the main activities (in this case, three main areas) for the after-school program they were thinking of implementing.

Outputs

Although inputs and activities tend to be components of the logic model that most people are quick to understand, **outputs** tends to be something that most have not thought about in such a way before. According to Frechtling (2007) outputs are "the immediate results of an action," or in this case an activity. In most cases, outputs are expressed numerically or are the immediate results of an activity occurring. For example, a group of teachers participate in online professional development training about the use of a classroom learning manipulative for students. Immediately following the training, the teachers fill out an exit survey. This survey quantifies changes in teacher beliefs about online training with teachers reporting that they found the training valuable and that it provided them with opportunity to pursue issues much more in depth than if they had been in face-to-face training. The teachers also reported that they plan to try the manipulatives they learned about in future classroom lessons. All of these benefits—a change in perception about online learning, the understanding that online learning can provide in depth coverage of content and material, and the potential for use of the manipulatives later on in their classrooms—are examples of outputs of the activity (i.e., online professional development) (see Figure 10.5).

  Another example of outputs focuses less on changing people's attitudes or knowledge and more about basic duties. For example, let's say that the activity is to purchase 100 new computers that teachers will eventually be trained to use. However, the actual output of the new computers is not teachers being trained; the more immediate result of purchasing the new computers is to get them set up and online, ready to be used. Although this may sound a little odd to be something that is depicted in a logic model, in reality such a basic function can be pivotal in the success of a much larger program designed to increase student writing through integrating technology into the classroom throughout a low-technology-ready school (see Figure 10.6).

Outcomes

Although we are not used to thinking about outputs of activities, we are accustomed to working with outcomes in education. Traditionally, **outcomes** are thought of as the end result of implementing a program or series of activities. In addition, outcomes are what we hope to achieve as a

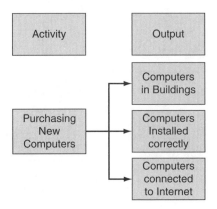

FIGURE 10.6 Outputs for Purchasing Computers

result of an effort. For example, an action research team might like student scores for ELA to increase on the state's annual standardized assessment, as in the case with Principal Johnson and Bryant Middle School.

However, a desired change in student performance or behaviors does not happen magically overnight. It takes time. In fact, some experts, such as Fullen (2006), report that such long-term changes typically take 5 or more years. A logic model requires its designers to not only focus on one type of outcome but also a series of outcomes existing in various degrees. In the logic model, this variation of outcomes is generally divided into short term, medium term, or long term. In general, short-term outcomes occur within 1 to 2 years of a program being implemented. In other words, what would be the outcome that the action research team realistically believes will occur at the end of the first year of implementation? The idea behind the short-term outcome is to begin to discourage us from the notion that the problem is going to be addressed in 1 year's time and that all students in the school are going to increase their performance. Medium-term outcomes occur in years 3 to 5. Short-term and medium-term outcomes may also be referred to as intermediate outcomes. In addition, long-term outcomes, or what is referred to as end outcomes, occur in year 6 and beyond. For example, changing student performance (e.g., higher scores) on the state's annual ELA standardized assessment might be the long-term or end outcome of a program.

Consider the preceding example with the desired end outcome being improvement in student performance on the state's ELA assessment. Prior to the end outcome occurring, many other components or events need to happen. In this example, teachers will have to logically change what it is they do in the classroom to improve their effectiveness. In this example, professional development might be used to help teachers improve their effectiveness by showing them how to integrate a series of research-based teaching strategies into their existing ELA lessons. In this situation, changes in teacher practices might be considered a short-term outcome. After a while with teachers successfully integrating these instructional practices into their instruction each day, students begin to grasp the concepts, materials, or skills being taught. An outcome of this new understanding of the materials might be increased student motivation, increased student interest in subject matter or learning in general, better class attendance or increased preparation for class, to name a few. Only after this increase in student learning on a daily basis would you then expect to see an outcome of students performing better on the state assessment (Stiggins & Duke, 2008).

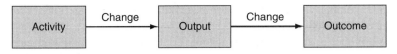

FIGURE 10.7 Theory of Change

SHOWING CHANGE WITH A LOGIC MODEL

As you begin to examine logic models, you will notice that they use arrows. These arrows show the theory of change or the ripple effect of the activity. Although the basic framework for a logic model is shown in Figure 10.3, in most cases logic models will include more than one resource, activity, output, and outcome.

Inserting arrows into the logic model should be purposeful since each arrow represents a change occurring, no matter how big or small. It is perfectly acceptable for several inputs to feed into the same activity. The same is true for every activity, as shown in Figure 10.7, as well as the relationships between outputs and outcomes, with every output being connected to at least one outcome.

Not everything included in the logic model has to be about change. There is also opportunity to show components of the model that have more to do with connections than a result or outcome. Connections are shown by the use of a line, as shown in Figure 10.8. A component of the logic model may have several connections. These connections clearly define the complex structures or workings of each section of the model. In this case, since they are activities, it would be correct to assume that in some way the logic model is suggesting these activities build on one another. In some cases, multiple activities can be connected with only one output taking place.

USING LOGIC MODELS

As noted, logic models first became popular in the field of program evaluation. Here they were used as a tool to measure the effectiveness of the program as well as a planning tool during the program's design and development. Even though you and your action research team are not professional evaluators, the logic model can certainly be an important tool and can fulfill many uses.

One of the most effective uses for the logic model is in the planning stage. At the same time you are gathering literature and school data on your topic, you can also be developing the logic model with your action research team. As you begin to work with it, your logic model can

FIGURE 10.8 Connections

serve as a guide, helping you and your team make solid logical connections between activities and the results of those activities.

The logic model is also an important tool for school leaders to use to gain a better, in-depth understanding of the thinking and perspectives of others. The logic model can help you as a school leader answer the question, How do others see the proposed activities that will eventually produce the desired outcomes for the project? The logic model can be seen as a puzzle. Understanding how others might put that puzzle of change together can be beneficial. Perhaps some of your staff or action research team members see the outputs of an activity or series of activities very differently from how you do. Perhaps they see outputs rolling out into different outcomes. This is important information for a school leader because it allows you the opportunity to understand how others see the process. For example, knowing that your staff sees the output of the professional development activity differently (prior to it occurring) may help you to either change it altogether, or modify certain elements, in order to create the desired outcomes.

USING THE LOGIC MODEL WITH YOUR ACTION RESEARCH TEAM

As noted, a logic model can be used in many different ways. It can be used as a framework to help in measuring and monitoring your schoolwide intervention (see Chapter 12). The logic model also can be used by the action research team to build your program. The most important thing to keep in mind when creating a logic model is that it should not be done in isolation, meaning that you, the school administrator, must not create the logic model in your office and then present it to the action research team. A better strategy, and one that will help build buy-in, is to have the action research team develop the logic model collaboratively.

Summary

Quality programs do not magically create themselves, they have to be developed and refined over time. Although a certain set of activities may seem like the logical approach to addressing an issue or problem that has been identified in a school, only a logic model can truly help show the connections between actions and outcomes. Although logic models have been used at state and federal levels, they have not, for whatever reason, been widely utilized for school improvement purposes. A logic model is a visual representation of how the activities (or actions) will relate to the final outcomes (i.e., resolving the identified school issue). Although there are variations of logic models in the literature, most logic models have the following basic parts: inputs, activities, outputs, intermediate outcomes, and end outcomes. It is recommended that the school leader work collaboratively with members of the action research team to develop a logic model. Experts in the field also believe that using logic models provides the same design as those experimental research designs that use a hypothesis to determine whether they have been successful or not.

Key Concepts

activities	inputs	outcomes
core activities	logic model	outputs

Discussion/Reflection Questions

1. In Vignette 10.1, Principal Johnston and the school community credited professional development with achievement of the end results: the ELA assessment scores going up. Develop a logic model for the vignette and, using the model, explain some of the reasons for what has occurred.
2. In examining the logic model in Figure 10.2 some may feel that the central seed for creating a ripple effect of change is showing teachers that technology will make their job easier: They will be able to manage materials, coursework, and assessments for students on home instruction much more effectively and efficiently than they have with the traditional paper trail approach. Be prepared to discuss why technology is considered to be such a key piece to change in this model.

Activity

1. As noted, logic models do not necessarily have to be displayed linearly like the one in Figure 10.1. In some cases, it is appropriate to show the logic model with a core (long-term outcome) in the center, with assumptions on the outside, followed by a band of inputs, activities, outputs, and short- and medium-term outcomes. Take the logic model in Figure 10.6 and rework it into a form in which a decrease in student dropout rates and improvement in academics are the core of the model.

CHAPTER 11

Step 4: Implementing the Program or Intervention with Fidelity

After reading this chapter you should be able to:

1. Understand the basic definition of fidelity in research.
2. Understand the different functions of fidelity in experimental research versus an action research study.

Vignette 11.1
The Action Research Team Implements Its Program

Principal Jones is working with her action research team to implement a new reading intervention in her school. Students who are two grade levels below in reading will participate in this "word attack" program once a day for 50 minutes. The program will run for the whole school year, giving students substantial exposure to the program. The action research team hopes that this intensive intervention will be just what low-performing students in ELA need.

In addition to setting up their study, the action research team also developed a logic model for it. In their logic model, they concluded that teachers would be trained in the program. Next teachers would devote one class period per day to the word attack instructional method. Students engaging in these activities would first begin to show changes in their fluency, followed by increased comprehension.

Principal Jones and the action research team have purchased all the materials for the teacher training and the program. They have hired a trainer to come in and train teachers on the program. After teachers are trained they begin to implement the word attack program in their classrooms. Before they begin to conduct observations of the program's implementation, members of the evaluation team design and develop a classroom implementation observation protocol. This protocol contains key variables or actions that the action research team would expect to see if the teachers were implementing the reading intervention correctly. To validate the protocol they use the professional judgment of literacy specialists on their action research team and in the school community. Once the protocol has been validated, members of the action research team go into classrooms and score the teachers in regard to the degree of accuracy in delivering the reading program correctly. To establish inter-observer reliability after the individual observations of classrooms, the scorers reconvene to compare their scores.

> At the end of the school year student performance on the chosen assessment shows mixed results. Some students have shown a significant change in their reading from the beginning of the year to the end of the year. The same results were not seen in other students. Members of the action research team examined their observation data for the classrooms with those students and found that those classrooms whose teachers had delivered the intervention correctly had students with greater gains than those classrooms where the intervention had been implemented in less than ideal ways.

WHAT IS FIDELITY IN ACTION RESEARCH?

Researchers who are studying the effectiveness of educational programs, interventions, and strategies often ask the question, "Was the independent variable (i.e., the program) implemented with fidelity?" Although this may sound a little strange, what they essentially mean is, *Is the program or intervention being studied correctly and to its full degree?* In a way, fidelity is a sort of quality control. It is important for researchers, particularly those who are conducting experimental and quasi-experimental research, to make certain that what they are studying is being implemented correctly. If the researchers do not determine the fidelity, and the results of the study reveal that the treatment made no difference than another treatment, one is not sure whether it was because the treatment had no ability to create the desired change or because it was never really implemented correctly (and therefore never had a real chance of making any change). Therefore, fidelity is an important component in cause–effect research, as shown in the example of the action research team studying the reading intervention.

Interestingly enough, fidelity is not something that we often think about in school as school administrators and leaders. Many times school administrators and leaders visit classrooms to observe teachers and instruction. In these situations, they are often conducting the observation for tenure purposes and are most likely doing so to observe the teacher for general instructional practices. Observations conducted for fidelity purposes are very different from those conducted for teacher tenure.

In Chapter 10, Principal Johnson provided teachers with new computers and all the training they could have wanted to integrate into their classrooms. However, if you recall, teachers didn't exactly use the technology in their classrooms. And if they did, they certainly didn't use it to the degree to which they were supposed to in order to bring about the increase in student writing and student performance on the state's ELA assessment. If the fidelity of the teachers' implementation of technology was checked by those in the action research team on a regular basis, team members would have realized the discrepancy and hopefully adjusted it accordingly by providing the teachers with a greater degree of support. This type of feedback is what is referred to as formative feedback in program evaluation. **Formative feedback** consists of the information or recommendations that are provided back to the participants of an activity to help scaffold or assist them in reaching their optimal potential during the activity.

In most research studies when no or low fidelity is discovered, the researchers document this by giving the setting (e.g., a particular classroom) a low fidelity score (e.g., a score of 1 out of 4). This low fidelity score factors into the study's results and allows for interpretation of those results in the final study. For example, if a study reports low fidelity for the classrooms where the study was being conducted and the results of the study were positive for supporting a particular program or instructional intervention, one might (and should) be skeptical. An experimental researcher, however, does not want to interfere with the process and provide formative feedback to those teachers who are implementing the treatment with low fidelity. If the researcher did this and the teachers modified their instruction to reach that level of fidelity (and the results from the study supported this new method), it would be impossible for the researcher to conclude that it was indeed the variables under study that made such an impact. After all, was it the combination of how the teacher was implementing the treatment with low fidelity along with how the teacher changed to implement it with high fidelity halfway through that ultimately made for a more effective treatment? If so, what was the treatment?

For the action research projects you would be doing with teams in your school, establishing fidelity for what it is you are studying is still critical; however, since action research is intended for more practical purposes, it would be acceptable for the action research team to provide the teacher or groups of teachers with formative feedback to help improve any settings where low fidelity of treatment was being documented. This feedback would also make it difficult for the action research team to determine what treatment students were receiving; improving teacher effectiveness in the classroom would be a number one priority and supersede the idea of avoiding extraneous variables.

DEVELOPING A FIDELITY CHECKLIST AND OBERVATIONAL PROTOCOL

Researchers conducting experimental research use fidelity checklists and protocols as a means of documenting whether fidelity is taking place in a study or not. In order to develop these fidelity measures researchers conduct a detailed process of identifying key characteristics and steps. Your action research team should conduct the following steps:

Step 1: Carefully examine any activity or treatment that is being given to students, staff, or any stakeholder group that is involved in the study. These activities would be the same activities that you have clearly delineated in your logic model. Action research members should know the treatment under study inside and out—whether it is a 20-week reading intervention or a series of instructional strategies that teachers will be implementing in mathematics or a new schoolwide behavior program.

Step 2: Next, the action research team will have to determine what the activities should look like. This does not mean *how* the activities should function but, rather, what they should look like if one was to observe them and say that they were being delivered to the highest level of implementation. In some cases, this may require members of the action research team to visit other schools in the district or other classrooms in order to see a program or intervention or instruction being conducted at a high level. From these observations, members of the action research team would then have to develop the observation protocols based on observing these high level implementations.

The criteria that make up the observational protocol are the key elements. Exhibit 11.1 presents an example of an observational protocol used for fidelity. Keep in mind that based on the project and its purpose, these protocols vary considerably.

Step 3: After the observation protocols are developed, the action research team would want to move about the school to conduct the necessary observations. It is important during the first steps of observation that the observers establish inter-rater or inter-observer reliability. **Inter-observer reliability** or inter-rater reliability is the ability for two individuals to observe the same situation and come to the same results or conclusions. In most cases, this involves the counting of observational traits or behaviors. For example, two individuals may use the same observational protocol and observe a classroom to determine the average number of off-task behaviors occurring in a 55-minute class period. In this example, one would want the two observers to come to about the same number of off-task behaviors at the end of the class. If this was the case, the two observers would have established inter-rater reliability between them.

EXHIBIT 11.1   Example of an Observation Fidelity Protocol

Criteria	Rating	Notes/Comments
Teacher moves around the room monitoring student work.	3 2 1 0	
Teacher provides adequate think time (4 seconds).	3 2 1 0	
Teacher delivers instruction at rapid pace.	3 2 1 0	
Teacher addresses student off-task behaviors.	3 2 1 0	

3 = Achieved, 2 = Developing, 1 = Beginning, 0 = No Evidence

Step 4: Once observer reliability is established the team members can move about while conducting their observations. Although the criteria and purpose of the observations will vary greatly, depending on the program under study, the essential process is the same. Observers should carefully record key information such as date, time, place, observers present, number of students, arrangement of rooms, and any other relevant information. In addition, observers should fill out a new protocol for each individual observation. Aggregating the data from the individual observations can be done along the way or at the end of the study.

When you are trying to determine the fidelity of your programs, it is important to understand that it may present you and the action research team with a dilemma—one that you will want to critically consider as a group before deciding how you will proceed. Consider the example in Vignette 11.1 of the action research team observing the fidelity of the reading intervention. In many of the classrooms, members of the action research team observed and documented (on their fidelity protocols) teachers who were not implementing the intervention to its highest possible level. Teachers in these classrooms may have skipped over important directions, muddled through parts of the instruction, missed key teaching points, mispronounced words, and so on. The dilemma is, *Do you as an action research team want to provide those teachers with formative feedback?*

Naturally, your action research team is trying to improve a practice in your school. It might be an actual instructional practice, but it also could be the procedures a teacher follows when disciplining a student and sending the student to the principal's office. Therefore, in the preceding example, action research team members might want to provide formative feedback to those teachers through a wide variety of methods, such as modeling, resources, videos, further professional development and training, and so on. However, as a member of the action research team you also have to remember that the formative feedback you provide (although we agree that this action is good and is at the heart of what you are trying to improve) is interfering with the results of the study.

As discussed, experimental researchers typically will calculate a fidelity score when observing teachers and classrooms. This score represents the degree to which the program or intervention was implemented correctly. The researcher would neither share this score with the person that was being observed nor provide formative feedback to that individual so he or she could self-correct their instruction, actions, or procedures. The researcher simply lets the individual do what he or she would naturally do, scores it, and uses that score in the interpretation of the results. Presumably, a classroom whose teacher was able to achieve low fidelity would not perform as well as on the final assessments as a classroom whose teacher reached high fidelity in the delivery of the program. You and your action research team will have to decide how you will use fidelity information within the formative process. Since the action research team's prime directives are to improve schools through improving the practices, procedures, and actions that take place within them, it is recommended that the action research team use formative feedback regularly. Since researchers are generally more hypothesis driven, the need to determine fidelity is usually more important than providing formative feedback.

EVALUATING PROFESSIONAL DEVELOPMENT

As noted in the preceding steps, professional development might be any activity that you and your action research team are proposing in your model. Although it is important to determine the fidelity of any professional development that may be occurring, the evaluation of professional development is oftentimes something that is overlooked in our schools today (Guskey, 2002). In many cases, not much data can be gathered about professional development, and therefore there is no real assurance about whether the professional development sessions were effective and made any impact or, more importantly for this chapter, delivered the key ingredient that the action research team deemed necessary in order to begin to address the school's identified issue or problem.

According to Green (2010), a school administrator has two ways to improve a school: hiring the best teachers he or she possibly can and retraining those who have already been hired. Since you and your action research team will most likely be implementing some type of new program or intervention across the school, you will also most likely be providing training to your teachers and related staff. Training is often necessary so that all involved stakeholders are aware of the purpose of the new project and understand the key components of the project, their roles and responsibilities, and how to go about doing "their part" to implement components with fidelity. For example, if the school is going to implement a reading invention to be delivered in the classroom, teachers who teach those grades will have to go through some type of professional development or training in order to be able to implement the intervention correctly. The same is also true about professional development for other types of interventions or programs you and the action research team may be implementing. Professional development (PD) can be informal or formal training to help teachers and related school staff to improve or change practices. Informal PD can consist of teachers working together to share practices during common planning times. Formal PD usually includes the expertise of an outside consultant. This consultant may work with large groups and or push directly into the classroom and model such practices for teachers.

For example, let's say your school is implementing a behavior program. Even though the program is not a specific set of rules as they would relate to instruction, there are goals and objectives that teachers and staff need to be informed of for the program overall, as well as a set of procedures to follow and knowledge that needs to be gained as to how the program works. Trainings on these specifics for teachers and staff can occur in different forms. In schools, much of the training needs to occur before the school year starts so teachers and staff are fully trained and ready to implement the program right away. In some cases, follow-up professional development trainings are also required (and recommended). These sessions would essentially be sprinkled throughout the project's period of implementation.

> **BOX 11.1 Examples of Level 1 Items**
>
> I found the presenter to be knowledgeable about the topic.
>
> I found the materials appropriate.
>
> I found the training to be well paced.
>
> I found the training to be worth my time.
>
> I found the room to be appropriate.

EVALUATING THE FIDELITY OF PROFESSIONAL DEVELOPMENT

The need to evaluate any professional development that occurs in relation to your program or intervention is intended to ensure that the PD actually takes place and that it was correctly executed. Without this assurance, one would not be able to determine whether the PD was truly effective in changing teacher practices and thus reaching the desired goals and objectives. This way, if the PD is delivered correctly, and those who participate in it deliver it correctly (with fidelity), one is able to better assess if it works. If any of the components break down during the process, it is impossible to determine what works and what doesn't.

When evaluating professional development, the action research team will no doubt have a long list of questions that they want answered: Is the PD high quality? Is it useful? Is the content of the PD correct? And what do participants (e.g., teachers, most likely) think about the PD? Take a minute and begin to brainstorm either by yourself, or with a small group of classmates, the types of general questions you would want answered if you were providing professional development training to teachers in your school.

After you have completed your list take a few minutes and begin to analyze what you have come up with. Do you see any patterns emerging among the items you have generated? Killion (2008), Guskey (2000), Kirkpatrick (1998), and Phillips (1997) developed a multilevel framework for evaluating professional development based on patterns or types of questions. The following are the various levels and their corresponding descriptions:

Level 1: These are basic questions presented to participants in a survey, interview, or focus groups. These items pertain to participants' reaction to the training and their overall satisfaction. Presented in Box 11.1 are some examples of Likert-type statements that would be considered Level 1 under this model.

Level 2: Level 2 items under this model pertain to measuring *a change or new knowledge* that has come about from participants engaging in the training. Information about this new knowledge can be collected through a wide variety of tools. Exit surveys from the training can contain a section pertaining specifically to items that assess participant perceptions of the new knowledge they have acquired as a result of participating in the professional development. Presented in Box 11.2 are examples of evaluation items that focus on Level 2.

Level 3: How many times have you participated in a training only to realize that you were not able to implement much of what you learned about due to lack of sufficient resources and support in your school? Level 3 focuses on evaluation of the impact of the PD on the organization itself and whether the organization and setting were able to adapt to meet the change in practice brought about through the PD. Again this could be assessed

> **BOX 11.2 Examples of Level 2 Items**
>
> I have gained a great deal of knowledge from the professional development.
> The professional development addressed all of my questions.
> After attending the PD session I have a better understanding of the main components of the program.

by the action research team through surveys, focus groups, and individual one-to-one interviews. Information pertaining to any challenges or barriers to implementing change within the organization should be used as formative feedback. Members of the action research team would want to use this feedback not only to rethink and realign their efforts but also to work to address these challenges and keep the action research project on schedule. To collect such data, members of the action research team would want to conduct routine observations of classrooms or everywhere else participants from the PD would be implementing their new knowledge and skills. Action research team members would want to document the changes in teacher practices that relate back to the key components of the PD. This is another opportunity for action research team members to provide feedback to teachers in order to address fidelity. This constant feedback and guidance will work not only to improve teacher practices in the classroom but also to maintain fidelity of what is being studied.

Level 5: Making the connection between PD and an increase in student performance is Level 5. In this level the evaluation efforts focus on documenting an increase in student understanding and behavior. Ultimately, Level 5 evaluation data work to determine if there are any notable changes in student classroom performance as well as on state and standardized assessments. Evaluation data for Level 5 can be student performance and records, interviews with teachers and students, and surveys and questionnaires.

Summary

Along with picking the program or intervention to improve your school, it is also important to make sure that the program (and its various components) are implemented correctly. Researchers refer to this as fidelity. Ensuring fidelity for your school's action research project is important for several reasons. First, when analyzing the program's outcomes, it is important to document that the program is being implemented correctly. If a program is found to be ineffective, it is important that the action research team rules out that the program was implemented incorrectly. A program is often made up of various activities or components. Observation protocols should be developed in order to determine the fidelity of the various activities or components. Members of the action research team should work collaboratively in documenting fidelity; however, in doing so team members should also work to establish inter-observer reliability.

Professional development is another common activity found in programs. To make a change in a school, typically the actions of others also need to change. This change can come through professional development; however, experts in the field have found that professional development often goes unevaluated. When evaluating professional development in your school, remember to do so through the five levels of professional development specified by experts in the field.

Key Concepts

formative feedback
inter-observer reliability

Discussion/Reflection Questions

1. Inter-observer reliability is noted to be an essential element in establishing fidelity for a program or activity. Why is this so important? What would be the limitations for the action research team findings if they do not establish inter-observer reliability?

2. Examine once again the five levels used to evaluate professional development. What are the benefits and challenges with findings that come about from each of these five levels?

Activity

1. Divide the class into five groups. Assign each group a level from the Kirkpatrick (1998) and Guskey (2000) models. Next, select a professional development session that needs to be evaluated. Have each group decide what method they would use and develop examples of items that correspond to one of the five levels. Groups should be prepared to present their method and items in class.

CHAPTER 12

Step 5: Gathering and Analyzing Data

After you have read this chapter you should be able to:

1. Understand the three levels of assessments data and their intended purpose.
2. Understand what constitutes a standardized assessment.
3. Know the three different types of standardized assessments.
4. Apply the three levels of data from assessments as well as the different types of measures to create a rigorous logic model.

GATHERING AND ANALYZING STANDARDIZED DATA

As discussed, schools today have no shortage of data at their disposal. In fact, many experts now report that schools have too much data—in fact, they are so inundated with data that they are unable to manage all of it, let alone use it in any meaningful way to drive school improvement efforts. Recognizing the amount of data available, experts are now encouraging school administrators and leaders to rethink what types of data they are focusing on (Stiggins & Duke, 2008).

THREE LEVELS OF ASSESSMENT DATA

Stiggins and Duke (2008) report that one of the problems with the current use of data is that school administrators and leaders treat all types of data as equal and don't see that data from various types of assessment may in fact have different uses. Data can be divided into three distinct categories: institutional accountability and policy-level assessments, program-level assessments, and classroom-level assessments (Stiggins & Duke, 2008) (as shown in Figure 12.1).

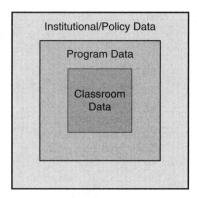

FIGURE 12.1 Overview of Three Levels of Assessment Data

Institutional accountability and policy level data are generated from the high-stakes assessments that students take annually. These data, often referred to as accountability data, are primarily focused on certain content areas (e.g., ELA and mathematics Grades 3–8) and high school competency examinations in the core content areas. According to Stiggins and Duke (2008), data from this level of assessment are used (or should be used) by policy makers, state level officials, and school administrators to make decisions about allocation of resources; however, in reality these data have been used to drive accountability, identifying schools whose students are not performing to certain benchmarks. These schools are then placed on improvement lists, slated for takeover by their state educational department, restructured, or closed.

Experts believe that data from this level of assessment have distracted many administrators and school leaders from focusing on critical aspects of student learning and performance. Instead, administrators have focused the time and energy of their staff on critically examining the assessments and conducting item analyses using descriptive and other low level analysis techniques. As you may recall, item, cohort, and longitudinal analyses of student data from these measures were done in the early steps of the action research process (initial data analysis for identifying the gap or issue in a school). Although these analysis techniques are appropriate and purposeful for identifying an issue that needs to be addressed during the early stages, they fall short when they are used as outcome measures.

Overall, institutional/policy assessments are summative in nature, telling how an individual or group performed. Data from these measures are not prescriptive; they do not provide information on what the individual or group now needs to do to address underperforming areas on the assessment or to improve on these deficits. In general, summative assessments are something like the old technology of taking pictures using film. A snapshot on film was an assessment of how the subject looked at a particular time on a certain day. And because it was taken on film that produced a negative there was little that most could do to change or improve the image—except, of course, to take another picture and hope for better results. Today, with digital cameras a picture can be taken and instantly seen, evaluated, assessed, and, with a plan, improved. Then we can make adjustments and take another picture. This process could go on indefinitely until we get the results we desire.

Institutional accountability and policy-level assessments are also akin to taking pictures with film. With such assessments, there is little we can (or should) be using to drive our instruction in the classroom, but unfortunately in many schools around the country this is exactly what we do. For example, if students do poorly on fractions or main idea, then we tend to work with the teachers of those students to consider how they taught those concepts and how they will change or alter their instruction the following year. In most such cases, the students who did poorly on items about fractions or main idea move on to the next grade, and the teachers change their instruction for a new batch of students. Yet the new students may come with the prerequisite skills and ability to master fractions or main idea in the way they had been taught before the items analysis took place.

In sum, one of the challenges with using institutional/policy data is that only snapshot data are provided. These data were acquired long before the students were learning what was assessed by the summative assessment, and therefore the data do not offer a solid foundation upon which to fully understand why students performed poorly on a set or series of items. Because of the divide between learning material and being assessed on it, changes often are made without any in-depth evidence or support to do so. Because of this, many schools find themselves in a constant state of flux. This flux can be confusing for staff as well as detrimental to overall morale in the school.

Program-level assessment data comprise the next level of data. Stiggins and Duke (2008) contend that this level of data is to be used by everyone at the school level, including but not limited to administrators, school and teacher leaders, teachers, and instructional support teams. These data allow those at the school level to examine and evaluate across multiple classrooms and work to improve school programming.

Program-level data would not be data that come from a high-stakes standardized state assessment, even though many use institutional/policy data to drive programming in their schools. Program-level data would come not from standardized assessments but from assessments that are more specially aligned with the programs and curriculum being implemented. For example, reading programs that are developed by larger publishers have "internal" assessments that all students in the school take periodically throughout the school year. In some cases these standardized measures are administered in the first part of the school year to assess students' reading ability, comprehension, and/or vocabulary levels. In some schools this is referred to as progress monitoring. However, no matter what assessments a school uses, administrators and school leaders should be using data from program assessments to measure the more immediate outcomes when a new program is put into place. They also should try to avoid focusing on the institutional-level data as the guiding light for determining whether or not their new program or intervention has successfully achieved their goal. The action research team should carefully include program data in their logic model and monitor closely as early evidence of success.

Data from **classroom-level assessments** can be developed and used by teachers in classrooms on a daily basis as formative feedback. Using our picture-taking analogy, classroom assessments would utilize digital cameras, providing the opportunity to take a picture of a student daily, analyze that picture, determine how to make it better, and then do so until the results meet final expectations. Stiggins and Duke (2008) note that this level of data is perhaps the most important level for school administrators, other leaders, and teacher(s) wishing to make changes in their school. They contend that if data collected on a daily basis from formative classroom assessments do not show student growth, then it is unlikely that the daily learning experiences for students would prove successful on the later summative assessment at the program or instructional-policy levels.

DIFFERENT TYPES OF STANDARDIZED MEASURES

In addition to the three levels of assessment data, three types of standardized measures or assessments are available to school administrators and leaders: norm group-, criterion-, and self-referenced measures (see Figure 12.2).

| Norm-Grouped Assessments | Criterion-Based Assessments | Self-Referenced Assessments |

FIGURE 12.2 Three Types of Standardized Measures

These assessment data comes from standardized assessments. A **standard measure** has a fixed set of questions/items, a fixed time frame and administration procedures, a fixed set of outcomes or traits being measured, and a referent through which an individual's score is interpreted (Lodico, Spaulding, & Voegtle, 2010). Before we do more in-depth analysis regarding how these measures could be used, let's begin by explaining how the three types differ in what they tell us about measurement.

Norm-referenced assessments are those standardized measures where an individual's score is not determined by the ranking of that score in the classroom compared to other students. Instead an individual's score is "interpreted" through how that student did compared to the norm. A **norm group** is a group of individuals who have already taken the measure. Their scores are used in creating a normal distribution. New scores on the measure are then interpreted through this normal distribution, like the one shown in Figure 12.3. Examples of norm-reference assessments include, but are not limited to, Gates-MacGinitie (Vocabulary/Comprehensive Assessment), California Achievement Test (CAT), TerraNova, Iowa Test of Basic Skills (ITBS) and Tests of Academic Proficiency (TAP), Metropolitan Achievement Test (MAT), and Stanford Achievement Test.

Criterion-referenced assessments are also common. In many cases, the high-stakes accountability measures are criterion referenced. For these measures an individual's score is interpreted not through a norm group but, rather, based on a set of criteria or standards. In most states' annual assessments, state learning standards are used. A student who demonstrated evidence of answering more items correctly also demonstrates that he or she has met or exceeded those criteria or state learning standards. Student raw scores are interpreted through scale scores. These scale scores (e.g., 450–558) are determined by the test developers, in addition to the cut score. The **cut score** is the point or score that separates those who meet the standards (i.e., pass the assessment) from those that do not meet the standards. Currently students who do not meet the cut score on state high-stakes assessments in English language arts (ELA) and mathematics receive academic intervention services (AIS).

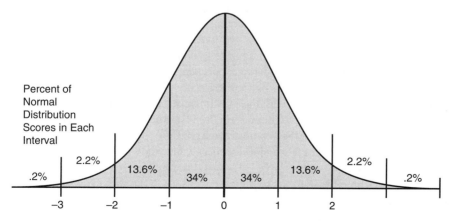

FIGURE 12.3 A Normal Distribution

One of the criticisms of criterion-referenced assessments is that the cut score is somewhat arbitrary and can be manipulated by a point or two in order to show student growth in a state. Recently, states have gone under scrutiny when their student performance on state assessments (criterion referenced) have continually improved over the last 5 to 8 years while their state scores on the National Assessment for Educational Progress (NAEP) (norm referenced) have remained the same over time.

Self-referenced assessments are the third type of standardized measure that administrators and school leaders work with on a regular basis. **Self-referenced assessments** do not base one's score on a norm group or criterion but on the individual's previous score. Self-referenced assessments are often given several times throughout the school year. An example of a self-referenced assessment is the AIMSweb.

Norm-, criterion-, and self-referenced measures can overlap with the three levels of data assessment noted by Stiggins and Duke (2008). For example, both a norm- and a criterion-based referenced assessment could be found as an end outcome. Many states use criterion-based assessments for their state testing accountability measure, and the NAEP uses a norm-group assessment to determine how students are doing from state to state. The same is true for program assessments. These can be norm grouped as well as self-referent in nature. Classroom-level assessments, which are standardized, should include one from across each of the different assessments: norm-, criterion-, and self-referenced.

HOW TO CRITIQUE STANDARDIZED MEASURES

When looking for different types of standardized measures, it is important to remember that just because a measure is standardized doesn't mean that it is a quality measure. Researchers refer to measurement quality as reliability and validity. Reliability is the consistency of the measurement tool used to get the same or close to the same score for an individual. It is an essential part of testing and measurement. For example, if an individual takes an IQ test and scores 120, then a week later the individual takes the same exact test again and receives a score of 80, the instruments would be said to be unreliable. A test that has sound reliability would give an individual the same score (or close to the same score) in this situation.

Several types of reliability should be established for standardized measures. **Test–retest reliability** is one such type. In order to establish test–retest reliability, the designers of the measure give the instrument to a sample. Then they let some time expire and administer the exact same test again (hence, test–retest). Finally, a correlation is conducted between the two scores for each individual. A test with a high correlation for test–retest shows that the measure is consistent with different administrations to the same person. A measure that is not able to show test–retest reliability during this phase would have to undergo further development.

Another type of reliability that standardized measures typically have is **internal consistency**. This is also referred in the literature as a split-half reliability. For this type, the test developers work to establish reliability or consistency with the instrument itself. Its purpose is to establish that the trait or construct being measured throughout the entire instrument is stable or consistent. To establish this, test developers administer the instrument to a pilot group, then literally split the test in half by separating odd from even items. Next, developers calculate the scores of each of the halves, then correlate the two scores.

Test developers are always trying to improve measures. One way to do so is to design them so it takes less time to administer them. When a new, shorter version of an assessment is developed, those who develop it look to equivalent-form reliability. In **equivalent-form reliability**, an older established instrument has to be available and is used to establish reliability for the new measure. The pilot sample takes both measures (which in theory are supposed to be measuring the same thing) and correlates each individual's score across the two tests.

Standardized measures should have validity established as well. **Validity** examines whether a measure is measuring what it intends to measure.

Content validity refers to whether the measure is measuring for the depth and breadth of the content and has two parts: item validity and sampling validity. For example, let's examine a high school biology exam. If you examine each item on the biology exam to make sure that the item is testing knowledge about biology, and not, let's say history, that would be **item validity**. **Sampling validity** does not have to do with examining each item for its relevance to content but has to do with looking at all the items that the test is measuring. Do these items reflect the entire year in high school biology, or do most of the items from the test focus on the last couple of months of class? In order to have sound sampling validity, the biology test needs to include items from across the entire school year. Test developers establish content validity through professional judgment bringing in experts who know the curriculum (in some cases, classroom teachers), and having them examine the depth and breadth of items.

Criterion-related validity is similar to what was discussed in Chapter 7 on correlational research. **Criterion-related validity** is established when one measure (the predictor variable) is used to predict what will happen on the second measure (criterion variable). In an educational context, criterion-related validity tries to show how accurate a student's score on the first test or measure will be for the second measure (a different form) without the student having to take the second measure. **Concurrent validity** is when the same form is used for predictive purposes.

Ultimately, test developers would like to establish construct validity for the measures. **Construct validity** is the highest level of validity. In many cases, it takes years to establish as well as a great deal of time, effort, and resources. In establishing construct validity, the test developers attempt to correlate their new measure with other established measures with which the literature says it should correlate. They also try to show that their new measure does not correlate with measures that the literature says it should not. In establishing construct validity, test developers might test their measure with as many as a hundred different measures over the course of its development.

CONFUSING RELIABILITY AND VALIDITY

Many people often confuse *reliability* and *validity*, using the two terms interchangeably; however, they both mean very different things. High-stakes assessments are often criticized for not being *reliable* measures. When people say this, they are typically referring to the fact that a high-stakes test a student takes on one single day might not accurately reflect that student's true knowledge and ability. After all, anyone can have a bad day; however, what they are referring to is not reliability but validity: truly measuring what the test intends to measure. In fact, it could be shown that the test was very reliable and that if a high-stakes test could be given to a student at two points in time (let's say a month apart) the student would get close to the same score on both administrations.

APPLYING DIFFERENT TYPES OF STANDARDIZED MEASURES TO YOUR LOGIC MODEL

Now that we have covered the basics of standardized assessments and their different types, it is time to think about applying what we have learned to our logic model. In previous chapters we have discussed basic components of a logic model: inputs, activities, outputs, intermediate

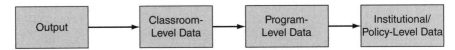

FIGURE 12.4 Applying Three Levels of Assessment Data into Your Logic Model

outcomes, and end outcomes; however, a great deal of rigor can be added to your logic model by embedding some standardized instruments into your logic model.

Take for example Stiggins and Duke's (2008) three levels of assessment data. Now think about applying those three levels into intermediate and end outcomes as presented in Figure 12.4.

In doing so you have created a more rigorous logic model by including outcome-like measures across a wide span of possibilities. In this example, in order for the action research team to take credit for the end outcomes occurring, the intermediate outcomes also have to occur. If the intermediate outcomes do not happen, then the action research team cannot accept the end outcomes being linked to the original activities, even if the end outcomes are met.

Another benefit of applying the three levels of assessment to the logic model is that it starts to provide members of the action research team with a framework to begin to think about data differently. Many times we only focus on end outcomes that consist of student data used for accountability. It makes sense. Recognizing the three levels allows team members, teachers, and leaders a broader perspective of what data are, what data can be, and most importantly how to use the right type of data for decision-making purposes.

By following the logic model presented in Figure 12.2, action research team members can begin to have conversations among themselves (and with teachers and instructional staff in the school) about what types of classroom and program-level data they should be collecting, what those data mean, how they will be interpreted, and how to use the different levels of data to shape their decisions as they work for ongoing school improvement.

Although institutional/policy and program-level assessments are standardized measures, classroom-level assessments in many cases may not be. In addition to adding the three levels of assessment data to your logic model, you can also think about adding different types of standardized assessment data to your logic model. As discussed previously in this chapter, norm-, criterion-, and self-referenced assessments are the three main types of standardized measures. Combining all three can dramatically improve the quality and rigor of a logic model.

Take for example the logic model presented in Figure 12.4. In this model, the action research team has put the ELA state assessment as the end outcome to their project. There is nothing wrong with this model; in fact, in many cases the end outcome for many schools and action research teams is to show an increase in their students' performance on state standardized assessments. However, one of the drawbacks of not having other standardized measures precede the end outcome is that the end outcome can be susceptible to extraneous variables. If you recall, test variability is one type of extraneous variable where the test itself fluctuates or changes. Perhaps one year items on the test are easier and everyone across the district, region, or state performs better on the assessment. Therefore, student gains on the assessment have nothing to do with students learning more or being able to meet a higher standard of performance. Including other standardized measures in the logic model will provide a sort of control within the model to gauge whether the end outcome achieved is due to real growth or extraneous variables.

For example, in the logic model presented below in Figure 12.5, the action research team has placed gains on the state's assessment in middle school mathematics as the end outcome. In

FIGURE 12.5 Improving Middle School Mathematics Logic Model

an early examination of their school data, the team found that students did not perform to the standard on the state assessment in math for several years in a row.

One subarea of the assessment noted for low student performance was proportional reasoning. Recognizing this, the action research team decided to implement a series of workshops for their middle school math teachers. These workshops provided teachers with an alternative method to teach proportional reasoning: through robotics. Teachers participated in six workshops and learned how to integrate robotics into their math classrooms.

The action research team knew that providing teachers with this type of professional development and predicting that student math scores would increase on the state assessment were unlikely possibilities. If such an increase did occur, there were reasons to doubt whether the work on proportional reasoning would have made that difference—particularly when presumably only a small portion of the state's mathematics test was made up of items dealing with proportional reasoning.

Recognizing this weakness with their logic model, the action research team set out to identify other standardized assessments to use. These additional assessments would not replace the state mathematics assessment as the end outcome but would be included in the model to help extend and support the findings. After reviewing many standardized assessments, the team decided to use the ARLIN Test of Formal Reasoning. Based on the work of Piaget, the ARLIN's purpose is to measure an individual's level (concrete, transitional, or formal) across eight subareas.

By adding the ARLIN, the action research team could now hypothesize that gains on students' ARLIN scores (particularly in the area of proportional reasoning) would be seen before gains on the state assessment. In fact, the team might be able to look only at individual items on the state assessment that measure proportional reasoning and not the gain on the entire test. This would allow them to draw a more logical link between activity (i.e., the workshop on robotics), the gains on the ARLIN subarea for proportional reasoning, and the gains on the state math assessment for items measuring proportional reasoning. Keep in mind, this is only if the robotics were actually adopted by the middle school math teachers and correctly implemented in their classrooms.

Summary

Collecting data is important for ongoing school improvement; however, knowing the limits of certain data sources is also important. Three types of assessment data are available to school administrators and leaders: institutional accountability and policy-level data, program-level data, and classroom-level data. Experts note that for too long school administrators have focused on using institutional accountability and policy-level data to improve student performance when, in fact, they should be using classroom-level data to support modifications in programs and curriculum. Aside from the three different levels of assessment data, it is also important to examine the three different types of standardized measures: norm-, criterion-, and self-referenced. In developing more rigorous logic models, school administrators and leaders should think about using different levels of assessments as well as different types of standardized measures.

Key Concepts

classroom-level assessments
concurrent validity
construct validity
content validity
criterion-related validity
cut score
equivalent-form reliability
institutional accountability and policy-level data
internal consistency
item validity
norm group
norm-referenced assessments
program-level assessment data
sampling validity
self-referenced assessments
standard measure
test–retest reliability
validity

Discussion/Reflection Question

1. As a future or current school administrator or leader, what benefits do you see with using a logic model to measure school improvement in your school? What might be some of the possible challenges? Develop a list for discussion in class.

Activity

1. Develop a list of program-level assessments that you currently use in your school. Examine each one, determine if they are standardized, and then develop a logic model for how you would incorporate them to improve the rigor of your logic model.

CHAPTER 13

Step 6: Reflecting and Making Modifications to the Plan

After reading this chapter you should be able to:

1. Understand how feedback loops are incorporated into a logic model.
2. Understand the difference between formative and summative feedback loops and how each can be used.
3. Understand how to reflect on activities, outputs, intermediate outcomes, and end outcomes to improve the action research process as well as the overall program being implemented in the school.

Vignette 13.1
Reflection and the Action Research Team

The action research team at Preston High School implemented a school-based mentoring program. The purpose of the program was to pair community members, as well as teachers and staff, with a high school student in need of an adult role model. Approximately 50 students in the school routinely got into trouble during the school day. The same students had high unexcused absences, office referrals, detentions, and suspensions. After reviewing the school data and the literature and research in this area, the action research team decided to implement a school-based mentor program.

The school advertised for mentors, and many volunteers from both the community and the school stepped up to help. Following a review and screening, the mentors received three training sessions. The first training session was designed to orient new mentors to the program and provide them with an overview of the program as well as the specifics of their role and responsibilities as mentors. The second session provided mentors with some initial activities that they could use during the first couple of weeks as they got to know their mentee. The third training provided mentors with some overview of academic and homework strategies they could use when working with their mentee on academics.

After the three trainings were completed, the mentors were assigned to their mentees and began their weekly meetings as required by the project's guidelines. At the end of the year the action research team examined the data in order to determine if the program was successful. Unfortunately, the end-of-year data for students who participated in the program was not encouraging. Students had approximately the same number of office referrals, days absent from school, and suspensions as they did before. When members of the action research team began to examine the program more closely they found that although the targeted students continued to be paired with a mentor at the end of the year, for many of the students their mentor had changed several times. In fact, one student's mentor had changed four times! Most of the community members who had initially volunteered and became mentors were no longer designated mentors at the end of the year, and most of the mentors were now teachers in the school.

"I'm not opposed to teachers and staff in the school stepping up and serving as a mentor," said Mr. James, a member of the team. "But our original plan was to involve the community and for our students to establish connections to people in the community."

"I wonder why community members didn't continue?" asked another team member.

"People are busy," replied Mrs. Smith, a high school English teacher and school leader on the team. "But I think we should try and contact some of the original mentors from the community and find out why they didn't stay involved. That way we know for sure."

Mrs. Smith divided the list of community mentors among the members, who contacted the mentors through e-mail. At the next meeting team members reported their findings. Team members reported that most of the community members wanted to mentor but after the third session didn't feel that they were prepared to do so. Many didn't think they had enough school-related strategies for working with the students on academics and would have liked to have more strategies that they could have incorporated into their mentoring sections. Many reported that they felt the students were challenging and that they (the mentors) didn't posses the ability or skills to work well with this population.

"If we would have known this after the third session," said Mrs. Smith, shaking her head, "we could have addressed it by giving the mentors much more support throughout the process."

The other team members agreed: Next time they would gather data throughout the process in order to address problems that developed along the way.

REFLECTING ON THE LOGIC MODEL TO DETERMINE SUCCESS

As discussed throughout this book, one of the major challenges with ongoing school improvement is linking school activities with the desired end outcomes. In our current educational system, gains or outcomes (e.g., high-stakes testing outcomes) are closely linked to what we do as administrators or school leaders; however, in reality the changes in outcomes may not be directly linked to the activities in the school. These changes in outcomes are often more related to other occurrences, often referred to by researchers as extraneous variables. You might also recall that the traditional method of linking activities in a school to increases in student performance on state standardized assessments is not only challenging but nearly impossible because of these extraneous variables.

Researchers try to address the issues surrounding extraneous variables by using a treatment and control group design to control for these extraneous variables; however, such designs are not often practical in school settings. Therefore, it is recommended that school leaders use logic models to make these important connections between the activities in a school and the results or outcomes that are being observed or measured (Frechtling, 2007).

In Chapter 10 you read about creating a basic logic model to serve as a guiding light throughout the implementation and monitoring of your program. In Chapter 12, you learned how to add a variety of assessment types to your logic model to increase the model's rigor and ability to filter out many of these extraneous variables.

Despite all of this hard work, it is important to remember that the logic model is a hypothesis (Weiss, 1997), a prediction of what you and your action research team believe is going to happen as a result of the new program and its related activities being introduced to your school. Since it is a prediction about the chain of events that will take place (Frechtling, 2007), it will need to be periodically reconsidered and modified as you work with it. You and your action research team will want to examine and reflect on your logic model throughout each step of the process—activities, outputs, intermediate outcomes, and end outcomes—and make the modifications to the logic model using both formative and summative data.

REFLECTING ON ACTIVITIES

The first step you and your action research team will want to take in the reflection process is to reflect on all the activities delineated in the logic model. It is important to make sure that the activities were implemented or conducted with fidelity. (Reexamine Chapter 11 for more in-depth information about how to do so.) If the evidence that you and your action research team members collect from activities reveals that the activities were not done with fidelity, then it is important for the action research team to address this gap. In some cases, this could be addressed by redoing or repeating the activity with participants or offering another method of delivery (e.g., deciding to replace a poorly attended training for teachers on literacy strategies with a series of webinars that teachers can either watch live or watch at a later date on a Web site). In other situations, the activity might need to be replaced altogether.

REFLECTING ON OUTPUTS

As you may recall from Chapter 11, outputs are the immediate results of engaging in a designated activity (Frechtling, 2007). In addition, you may recall the importance placed on the action research team measuring the outputs of any activity. It is also very important for the action research team to critically reflect on this output data in order to determine whether the activity has been successfully achieved.

Taking the preceding webinar example, output data would most likely consist of information from those teachers who participated in the webinars, how satisfied they were with the webinars, and whether they learned anything and plan to move forward by implementing what they learned into their classrooms. This output data would most likely consist of survey data gathered from teachers after participation in each webinar (see Figure 13.1). In addition to survey data, the action research team might wish to collect interview or focus group data from teachers after the webinars.

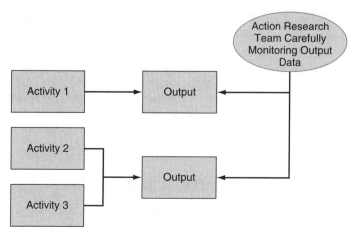

FIGURE 13.1 Overview of Output Data

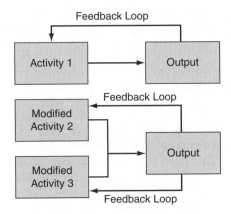

FIGURE 13.2 Example of Outputs with Feedback Loop

It is important for the action research team to critically examine the output data for each session in order to determine participant satisfaction with the webinars, as well as any potential challenges participants might report as to why they cannot implement what they have learned. In the logic model such formative data collection can be depicted with what is called a feedback loop.

Feedback loops indicate where the action research team anticipates informative data will be collected. In Figure 13.2, a feedback loop has now been added to the logic model using webinars to deliver professional development (PD) to teachers on literacy strategies. It is important to keep in mind that feedback loops should not be an afterthought but should be incorporated into the logic model as it is being developed; however, it is perfectly acceptable for the action research team to decide that a feedback loop is necessary and add one at any time during the action research process.

In reflecting on the output data, the action research team must determine whether the outputs have been met and where the program implementation can move forward. Continuing with the webinar example, let's say that the teachers were not satisfied with all of the webinars that were created and had reported serious concerns about them on the surveys provided by the action research team. In addition, the teachers reported that they anticipated many challenges were they to try and implement the literacy strategies they had learned about through the webinars. Reflecting on this information, the action research team would have to decide if additional webinars would help to address the concerns brought up by the teachers in the outputs data or whether they should change to a different modality altogether and institute a new series of traditional face-to-face trainings. In determining this, the action research team would have to modify its original activities in order to accommodate staff needs and present the highest quality possible of activities and their usage by teachers. Figure 13.3 shows how the logic model could be modified to reflect these new ideas.

REFLECTING ON INTERMEDIATE OUTCOMES

After reflecting on outputs, it is time for the action research team to think about looking critically at intermediate outcomes. As previously discussed, intermediate outcomes can be either formative or summative in nature, depending on the nature of what is being studied by the action

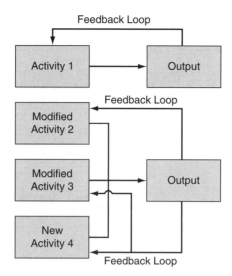

FIGURE 13.3 Change in Logic Model Following Reflection

research team; however, what is important is that the action research team critically examines intermediate outcomes to determine if they have been met, partially met, or not met at all.

Take again the logic model in Figure 13.2. The intermediate outcome of the activity (i.e., webinars) is teachers beginning to implement the literacy strategies that they learned through participating in the webinars. This evidence could be gathered through multiple methods, including but not limited to surveys, interviews, focus groups, reviews of lessons plans, student projects and work, classroom assessments, instructional materials, and direct observations of the classroom by members of the action research team. If data from the intermediate outcomes do not reveal teachers implementing the strategies, then the action research team must reconvene and discuss how to increase implementation. In this situation the action research team may find two different groups of teachers participating in the project. They may find some enthusiastic teachers participating in all the webinars and actively working to integrate as many of the strategies from the webinars as possible. Unfortunately, they might also find some teachers who are less enthusiastic about the webinars and the strategies and show little evidence of implementing the strategies in their classrooms. In addition to teachers implementing what they have learned, other intermediate outcomes might focus on changes in student learning in the classroom related to teacher-developed measures. These would include but are not limited to student work and projects, quizzes, class assignments and homework, unit tests, and any other measure a teacher may use to assess student learning (see Figure 13.4).

Regardless of what intermediate outcomes you are using, it is important that your action research team critically examine and reflect on the data from intermediate outcomes. Data from these feedback loops would most likely go back to activities and could be used as formative data by the action research team to evaluate the activities for next year's program or, if time permits, for implementation of new activities that address the issues noted in the intermediate data.

For example, in the case of webinars, if the intermediate data reveal that teachers are not implementing the literacy strategies or are implementing the strategies incorrectly, then the action research team may decide to develop a new webinar. This new webinar (which was not originally planned for) would focus on what teachers should be aware of when implementing the strategies (i.e., the do's and don'ts).

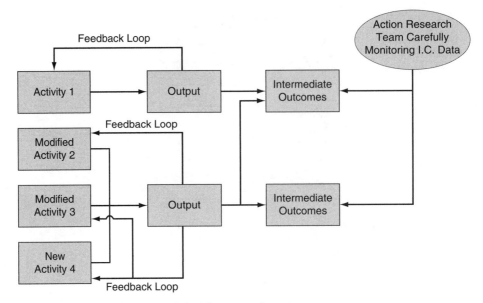

FIGURE 13.4 Overview of Logic Model with Intermediate Outcomes

REFLECTING ON END OUTCOMES

Examining and discussing data from end outcomes is something that many individuals in schools are familiar with and comfortable doing. As discussed in previous chapters, school teams are often assembled at the end of the year to examine and reflect on how students performed on annual state standardized assessments. The teams divide items into subareas and use this item analysis to plan for next year's PD or the school's program planning effort. Unfortunately, much of those efforts is done without a context or plan in place. Without a plan (i.e., logic model), school administrators and leaders will draw cause–effect conclusions that may be incorrect. Thus, they believe their efforts are supporting an improvement in their end outcomes, when in fact they are not.

In Figure 13.5 the action research team is reflecting on the end outcome data. In doing so the team also has to take into consideration the data from activities, outputs, and intermediate outcomes. Notice in Figure 13.5 that the action research team cannot claim credit for the end outcomes occurring when the other components of the logic model were not also met. Outputs and intermediate outcomes that were not successfully met along the way are symbolized in Figure 13.5 by dashes.

For example, if the action research team did not see the outputs expected from the activities (i.e., teachers not implementing the strategies in their classrooms), then they cannot attribute the changes on the end outcomes (e.g., student scores increasing on the state's ELA assessment). The idea or logic behind this method of thinking is that the scores on the test could not have increased because the literacy strategies were never implemented; therefore, the increase in student performance on the ELA assessment must be due (or in part due) to one or more other variables. For example, if your school's goal was to improve student achievement in ELA scores and your school's ELA scores did improve that following year, can you attribute this to you and your action research team? Can you attribute it to anything? The only way that you can attribute it to

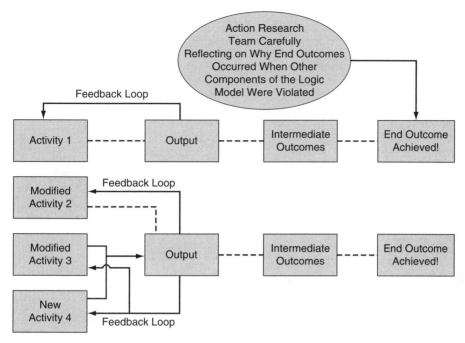

FIGURE 13.5 Reflecting on End Outcome Data

the activities that you have chosen in your logic model is if the components in the middle were also met. In other words, were the outputs from the activities achieved? Were the intermediate outcomes achieved? If they were not, then you have violated the theory of change that you had predicted during the creation of your logic model. If you and your action research team are going to be truly guided by your logic model, then you would not be able to take credit for the improvement in ELA scores. Even though there is no way to determine this for sure, the changes in ELA scores are probably due to other extraneous variables that are present in your school and the entire testing community as a whole.

It should be noted, however, that feedback loops used to collect formative data might successfully address outputs and intermediate outputs the second time around. If this was the case, and these components were examined and successfully met, then the action research team could take credit for the final changes in end outcomes.

In addition, it is possible that the logic model is incorrect and that the results being seen are indeed the results of the action research team's labor. It is also possible, however, as in the preceding example, that the action research team would have to reflect on the old logic model. The team would have to decide what the new outputs of the activities were and what the new intermediate outcomes that had affected the results of the ELA scores were. This process may seem simpler than it really is. Reexamining and correcting a logic model is difficult in that there may be no new outputs or intermediate outcomes that members of the action research team can provide that make the logical connections to the end outcomes improving (i.e., ELA scores). If this is indeed the case and the logic model cannot be modified to create a new pathway to explain the chain of events, then the action research team would have to assume that the gains were made by extraneous variables.

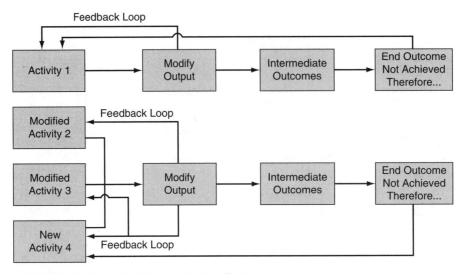

FIGURE 13.6 Example of Summative Feedback Loops

Summative feedback loops, which are similar to formative feedback loops, can also be used. **Summative feedback loops** are connected to end outcomes data. As shown in Figure 13.6, the summative feedback loop serves as an indicator to remind the action research team members to reflect on the entire process and continually make yearly reflections on the entire logic model.

THE ACTION RESEARCH TEAM AND MAKING MODIFICATIONS

Using the logic model as a tool for reflection is just one of many ways the action research team can benefit from the action research process. As the school leader, it is important to remind members of the action research team that the logic model isn't something that they should formulate, check off their list, and leave in a desk drawer or filing cabinet. The logic model should be a collaborative, ongoing document that is constantly modified and refined during each reflection. You and your action research team should also think about keeping the original draft of your logic model and making subsequent changes on another copy. In doing this, the original can be compared to what the final logic model becomes at the end of the process. It is unlikely that an action research team's original plan would look exactly like the final logic model at the end of any project. Although the action research team has reviewed and used the latest research to develop a model to address the identified school-level issue, because of the unique features of each school, context, and setting, even the best laid plan is going to experience some setbacks and modifications and will require tweaking to successfully address a school's needs.

Summary

Reflecting on the logic model is an important process if action research teams are to be successful. Feedback loops are used in the logic model to indicate where the action research team needs to stop and collect data during the action research process. These feedback loops can be both formative and summative, depending on the data that are being collected. Formative feedback loops link data from outputs back to the activity and require members of the action research team to critically examine whether the activities have been conducted correctly. Summative feedback loops tend to link end outcomes data (and in many cases data from intermediate outcomes) back to the activities that have been conducted. If activities have not been correctly implemented, and outputs and intermediate outcomes are not in place, then the action research team cannot attribute end outcomes being met since they have not successfully addressed the changes that they predicted would occur between the activities and the end outcomes.

Only by reflecting on the data that are being gathered throughout the action research process can members of the action research team truly modify and refine the activities or programs that have been put in place to address school-level issues successfully.

Key Concepts

feedback loops
summative feedback
    loops

Discussion/Reflection Questions

1. How is reflecting with the logic model similar to and/or different from the ways school leaders and school teams typically use data to drive school improvement?
2. When using the logic model, it is important that if end outcomes are reached, all the other components in the model are also reached. When this is not the case and you achieve end outcome without achieving outputs or intermediate outcomes, your end outcomes become suspicious and are most likely occurring for another reason. Take a minute to think about what extraneous variables might be generally present in your school and play a role in all of this.

Activities

1. Pick a particular issue in your school and a program that you would like to implement to address it. Develop a logic model that you and your action research team (if you had one) could use to guide the project. Then add formative and summative feedback loops to your model to indicate areas where data and reflection would occur.
2. For the project that you have developed in question 1, develop a list of the various tools (e.g., surveys, protocols, assessment data) that you would use to collect both formative and summative data using your feedback loop. Be prepared to present your logic model, feedback loops, and list of data collection tools in class.

CHAPTER 14

Case Study 1: Addressing High Teacher Turnover and Low Student Performance

BACKGROUND AND PERSONAL CHARACTERISTICS OF A SCHOOL LEADER

Maria St. James is the acting principal of Girls Can Learn Inc., an urban charter school. This is her first position as a school administrator, but after only a few days into the new school year, staff begin to describe her as competent, eloquent, and highly reflective.

Girls Can Learn Inc. has been in existence for the last 5 years. Maria accepted the position in the summer of 2010 and over the summer began to examine more of the school's performance data. Although this is her first administrative position after receiving her teacher and district license, she is more than ready to apply both the theoretical and practical knowledge she learned in graduate school to improve her failing school. Unlike many of her fellow students, Maria sees a strong relationship between the course work she took in graduate school in education leadership and the day-to-day position of a school administrator.

"There is absolutely a strong connection," says Maria. "What I have read and researched, based on the assignments professors gave me to read, has been valuable on an ongoing basis as I work to evaluate teachers."

She also notes that her experience of the professors who were delivering the material also was critically important. "I do not like sitting in front of a professor [and you see this all the time] who only has a couple of years of experience in the field. But I have to say that at The Institute, I didn't find this; all the professors had a wealth of experience that allowed them to have a critical perspective that they were then able to deliver to me in the classroom. I found it quite refreshing, actually."

In addition, Principal James brings a different perspective to the classroom. When she took graduate courses she was not like most of the potential school-leaders-in-training, as she was already an acting principal at Girls Can Learn Inc. She explains how this unique situation provided her with an opportunity to learn, reflect, and apply much of what she was learning in the classroom.

"It [the courses] was an overwhelming experience. I loved it [the courses]. I loved the research that was being presented. But it was a little overwhelming because I was working as an actual principal at the same time. However, I was also at an advantage because *I was living it! There were no what if's. This was it!* I was able to see it and apply it, as a professional." Principal St. James added that, unlike many of her classmates, she did not have to think about how to apply what she was learning down the road. She could go to school the next day and start working on it. She felt this gave her a more powerful connection to the material and elevated and made the experience more meaningful.

Principal St. James also points out that not all learning in her classes came directly from professors' lectures. A lot of learning, she says, comes from students (i.e., other future principals) from the public school sector trying to learn more about charter schools, and in many cases trying to break down the misperceptions they hold about charter schools.

"A lot of my classmates were misinformed about the funding for charter schools. They may not have agreed with the funding [stream], but they were very misinformed. They also were misinformed about what goes on operationally; they were misinformed about the accountability on our level. For example, they thought that we [charter schools] don't take the state test." Principal St. James said that she used the class discussions to educate her classmates about charter schools: their purpose, their mission, and the student population they serve. She says that she believes that the students in her graduate classes may not have all walked away from embracing charter schools, but at least they walked away with a more accurate and better understanding of them.

When the discussion focuses on student achievement and accountability, Principal St. James is acutely aware of the issues facing her teachers and students. She credits course work in EDA 503 Curriculum, EDA 510 Supervision, and EDA 585 Supportive Learning Communities with providing her with some of the techniques and skills needed to work with her staff and make her school as effective a learning environment as possible. Through her course work, she now fully understands the important role that supportive learning communities play in a school administrator's success. She also sees how charter schools are perhaps better suited to provide those supportive learning communities. For example, she asks her teachers how they [as a team] are going to change the face of their literacy program and if they have any ideas. She believes one of the benefits they have, as a charter school, is the freedom to think and investigate and decide what is best for students and their optimal learning. As a charter school, there is no talk about contracts keeping teachers from working to improve instruction.

STEP 1: FORMING THE ACTION RESEARCH TEAM

Armed with her theoretical and practical knowledge and seeing a strong connection between course work and practice, Principal St. James is ready to address the major problems of the building: academic achievement and teacher turnover rates. Principal St. James understands the importance of fostering relationships with staff and building community, and she realizes that creating a building-level action research team is the perfect opportunity to do so. The prime directive of the team is to examine data, identify the root causes of the issue, determine the most promising approach to address the issue, and monitor and refine the action plan as they work with it. Principal St. James selects a teacher from each of the grade levels, along with the school psychologist to serve on the team.

In addition, since she wants to be an active (but equal) part in the shared decision-making process, Principal St. James decides that she will play a participatory role in the action research process. To do this, she will serve on the team alongside the other members of her staff. As part of the participatory role, Principal St. James will have a voice on the team, but her voice (or ideas) will have no more weight than any of the other members of the team.

Reflecting back on the team experience, Principal St. James notes that it was a little more challenging than she had originally thought it would be. "In my course work and classes, I had learned the importance of having a voice and having everyone on my team have an equal voice. It's funny because we talk about that in theory, but in practice it is a whole different story." Principal St. James explains that it was difficult for her to take a back seat and listen to her staff's thoughts and interpretations of data or the cause of the problem, particularly when she did not agree with their analysis.

"I found it helpful to hear everyone's thoughts about the issue," says Principal St. James. "In the end I think it provided me with a good foundation as to where people were coming from."

Another challenge when working with her action research team was that staff were not able to completely transform into the new role. Principal St. James notes that staff also were hesitant to express their opinion, and at first seemed to tiptoe around the issue during discussions. In addition, staff often seemed to acquiesce to Principal St. James, believe that her opinion or perspective was the reigning one, and not realize that they all had an equal say on the issues. Principal St. James notes that sorting out everyone's new role and responsibilities on the team took a while, but members of the team were eventually able to assume their new positions.

STEP 2: CONDUCTING THE DATA ANALYSIS

After the team had been established and the ground rules laid out, Principal St. James's action research team quickly got down to work on one of the most important components of the action research process: data analysis. The team began to examine the data that were most accessible to them: student performance data on the state's annual assessment. Table 14.1 presents student performance data for Grades 3 and 4 on the English language arts (ELA), mathematics, and science assessments.

Table 14.1 Girls Can Learn Inc. State ELA/Math/Science Scores

	2006–07	2007–08	2008–09	2009–10
ELA				
Grade 3	23*	25	25	19
Grade 4	33	32	18	22
Math				
Grade 3	84	66	81	100
Grade 4	76	43	88	100
Science				
Grade 4 (only)	10	22	7	0

* Percentage of students passing

As part of the initial data examination process, team members discussed their ideas and thoughts about the data, why the data is the way that it is, and how they think it could be improved.

"Clearly, there is a great need to improve student performance in all the content areas," said Mrs. Jackson, a fourth-grade teacher who has been at Girls Can Learn Inc. since it opened its doors 5 years ago. "Each year they keep bringing us more and more kids who come to school without the skills they need to have to be successful."

"I agree," said Mr. Halt, a third-grade teacher who joined the staff the year before. "There are academic and personal skills that I just assumed students had coming into third grade, but many of our students just simply do not possess them. So I have to start teaching them, trying to help them catch up, and they just never do."

"We can't overlook the parents," said Miss Walker, a fourth-grade teacher in her first year. "Parents are a big part of the problem. I can't tell you how many parent–teacher conferences I have here in this school, and the parents come in and act no better than the student. How can we do our job if parents don't do theirs?"

"Look at these scores!" replied Mrs. Jackson. "Not a single student in fourth grade passed the state's science assessment last year. That is just depressing. Not a single student." Mrs. Jackson kept shaking her head and combing through the pages of tables and data in the folder in front of her.

"I think we need to have some kind of parent program," said Miss Walker. "We can only do so much in the classroom. We need parents to meet us halfway if we are ever going to get students' scores to improve."

"I think we need to examine the reading curriculum that we currently use here," said Mr. Halt. "Because students are coming in much more deficient in early literacy, I think we need to take a serious look at how we teach reading here."

Hearing the discussion before her, Principal St. James was surprised that no one had brought up other important variables. After letting everyone on the team talk, Principal St. James decided to add her perspective. "What about the high teacher turnover rate in the school?" She handed out another sheet of data, this time with the teacher turnover rates for the last 4 years. Table 14.2 presents the turnover rates.

"Wow, I knew it was high, but I never knew it was this bad," interjected Mrs. Jackson. "I know I am the only one around from the group of teachers hired with me."

Everyone else around the table chimed in. They too acknowledged the fact that most of the staff that were hired alongside them had moved on and left the school. As a group, they also acknowledged that the transient rate of their teacher populations played a pivotal role in the success and sustainability of their school. The constant flow of teachers in and out of the school made it difficult to implement curriculum with fidelity, create an institutional memory, or develop any kind of professional or learning community. Collectively as an action research team, the group decided to first address the alarming teacher turnover rate.

Table 14.2 Impact of Principal St. James' Leadership on Teacher Turnover Rate

School Year	2005–06	2006–07*	2007–08	2008–09
% of Teachers Leaving	64%	69%	25%	25%

* When Principal St. James arrived at the school

STEP 3: CONDUCT A REVIEW OF THE LITERATURE

Consulting with her school-level action research team, Principal St. James knows that the next step in the action research process is for the members of the action research team to begin conducting a review of literature on addressing teacher turnover rates.

The team decides to divide the work up among themselves, and each team member agrees to gather five articles from the literature on addressing high teacher turnover rates in a school. Next, each team members carefully reviews the articles and presents them to the team.

YOUR TURN . . .

Pretend that you are a member of the action research team (or the team itself if you are working in a group). Next, gather five research studies from the literature on teacher turnover rate and apply the basic analysis template found on in Chapter 6 to pull out the key bits of information. Then prepare a short presentation summarizing all the documents and the key points of each. Make your presentation to the class or action research team.

STEP 4: COLLECTION OF ADDITIONAL DATA FROM STAKEHOLDERS

In addition to the review of the literature, members of the action research team also decided that they needed to collect information from the current teaching staff. The team decided that an anonymous survey would be best for collecting valid data and then began to brainstorm about some broad questions that they would like answered.

"I am curious why people come and go here?" asked Mrs. Jackson. "I have been here for years. I think this is a pretty nice place to work, and the teachers are good to work with. I am wondering why people leave."

"I am wondering if there is anything that we could do to address the issue or further support teachers so that they will stay," said Principal St. James.

For the next 30 minutes the team continued to generate broad research questions. They then planned to take these broad research questions and generate a short survey. They planned to administer the survey to teachers and use the data as another source of information (along with school data and what they discovered in the review of literature) to help form their final decisions on the action plan they will put in place in hopes of addressing the high teacher turnover rate in their school.

YOUR TURN, AGAIN . . .

Pretend that you are a member of the action research team or, if you are already working in a group, that you are the action research team. Take a few minutes and begin to brainstorm ideas and broad questions that you would want to ask teachers and staff in your school regarding the high turnover rate. Develop a short survey to give to your staff. Be sure that the survey uses Likert-type items and other appropriate scales to ensure that those filling it out can do so as easily as possible. Also, discuss how you are going to disseminate the survey to the teaching staff and how you will be collecting it. Be sure to consult Chapter 9 in order to review procedures regarding validity of the survey data. Present the final survey to the class.

CHAPTER 15

Case Study 2: Decreasing the Performance Gap Between General Education and Special Education Populations

BACKGROUND AND PERSONAL CHARACTERISTICS OF A SCHOOL LEADER

Assistant Principal Leslie Bakersfield is a committed individual. She is confident, reflective, and has a deep understanding of special education and how to best serve high school students that are identified with special needs. Although this is her first position as a school administrator, she is not new to education and the challenges that come with the position. Before attending graduate school and getting her teacher and district leader certificate, she was the Committee on Special Education Chair for a nearby district and had over 20 years of experience in education.

When Ms. Bakersfield took the position as assistant principal with a focus on special education, she knew exactly what she was getting herself into. Ms. Bakersfield had been involved in special education for her entire school career. She says that she has been the assistant principal of the high school for 2 years now and that this is the longest anyone has ever stayed in this particular job. She says that this high turnover rate for the position is a testimonial to just how bad the disconnect with relationships had been in this school.

"It has really been a tricky job, and I would have to say that last year was really bad. This year has been much better, and it has been going much better, and I just think there had been a variety of reasons," she said during our first interview with her.

Ms. Bakersfield brings to the school a wealth of resources and knowledge about special education and the use of data. One of the main things Ms. Bakersfield has focused on is working with school personnel to collect and analyze data. Observations of work sessions conducted over the course of the last 2 years reveal that Ms. Bakersfield has played a major role in working with staff to use data more effectively for ongoing school improvement.

Springfield is a suburban district. Most of the Springfield City School District's population comes from families with middle- to high-income jobs. The Springfield City School District compares favorably in instructional expense per pupil when compared to other similar districts. According to the *State School Report Card Fiscal Accountability Supplement,* the Springfield City School District spent $8,228 in instructional expense per pupil in 2005–06. This is comparable to the average $8,399 for similar districts. There are approximately 8,000 children in the school district, with about 15% of those children meeting the requirements for free or reduced lunch. The Springfield district operates eight schools to serve its students, which includes six elementary schools, one middle school, and one high school. Attendance is good at all schools, with an approximate rate of 96% of students in daily attendance, and Springfield's suspension rate is lower (approximately 3%) than many other similar districts.

The population is mainly White (approximately 93% of the student body), but the district does have a small percentage of Black students (approximately 4%) and Hispanic students (approximately 1%). There also is a small population of students who are of Asian and other designations (approximately 1%). Also within the school population, approximately 25% are limited English proficient students.

Ms. Bakersfield knows effective leaders rely on data to make decisions, and she has worked with staff to try and scaffold them to think the same way. Ms. Bakersfield says, "For example, teachers will say I have students stay after school all the time and that should help, but no one has ever collected data stating who stays after or how often they stay, so we have been gathering data and we do a monthly report to the school board, compiled by the principal and myself, on what exact strategies we are using; what data we have collected; and how we are making strides in equitable scheduling, making sure ratios are appropriate in co-taught classes, that teachers are getting the right amount of professional development, etc. It's been a big, big process. As far as classroom instruction, I obviously do observations, teacher observations, and professional development, and the unique thing is I do not just observe special education teachers, I observe general education teachers all the time and help provide them, when they say they need something, to help make their co-teaching experience better. I try to provide that and get them what they need."

LEVEL OF PREPAREDNESS

Ms. Bakersfield found her course work in her graduate program to be very beneficial. "I felt really confident coming into this position that I could handle anything that was thrown at me, based on the course work," she said.

She also found courses that involved data to be beneficial. "Definitely, the data course really helped. I came in knowing what a professional community is, what the lingo and jargon were, and if I don't know what it is I know who to contact—I have contacts of people who I know will help me. The program was awesome; I wish I had done it ten years earlier in my career. I wish it would have been around earlier."

Ms. Bakersfield says that one challenge she faces is getting staff members motivated to improve their craft. "I don't know how to teach old dogs new tricks. That's what I think has been the hardest thing. Professional educators don't keep up on what is out, current issues. I think teachers need refresher courses here and there. Once they get tenure, they just remain static, though that is not true of all teachers; but some do not want to change," she says.

She also says that even in 2009, she is still going out into the field and training teachers on what an Individualized Education Plan is. "That amazes me," she says. "It is so frustrating, and I am not talking about all older teachers. I am talking about some of the newer, younger teachers just fresh out. They do not want to know anything about that special education piece. Institutions of higher learning have got to start teaching people about students with disabilities," says Ms. Bakersfield.

PROFESSIONAL DEVELOPMENT/STAFF. Ms. Bakersfield also has worked to find professional development opportunities for her staff. "I have done lots of implementations for my staff. I have not gotten as much as I would like. Last year, I did get to go to a two-day conference. And I really, really liked that, and I would like more, but unfortunately I have not gone to one conference this year. I think it's a combination of budget issues and that I think they feel they need me here. I guess. I don't really know. But I would like more than that," she said.

SUPERVISION. In addition to those responsibilities, Ms. Bakersfield also is in charge of conducting teacher observations and evaluations. She says that she especially enjoys doing the special education observations because she is confident with that learning environment. She says that observations of general education classes are a challenge because she is not familiar with the content. "Good teaching is good teaching, but lack of content in a field can certainly hamper one's ability to conduct valid observations," she notes.

STEP 1: FORMING THE ACTION RESEARCH TEAM

As she begins to follow the action research cycle, Ms. Bakersfield knows that her first step is forming an action research team to examine issues across the high school, as well as the district. In forming her action research team, Ms. Bakersfield carefully selects a group of high school teachers who she thinks will work well together and bring a wide variety of perspectives to the table. Ms. Bakersfield selects seven other individuals to serve on the action research team: the school psychologist, two special education teachers, three content teachers from the high school (English, mathematics, and science), and a parent. She feels that this group will be able to carefully examine and work with the existing data in the high school and develop a plan of action that will not only work to address the issue at hand but do so through a unique perspective.

STEP 2: CONDUCTING THE DATA ANALYSIS

One of the first two data sets that the action research team examines is the school's state assessment data for English language arts and mathematics. Table 15.1 presents the results of the high school data for general education and special education students for the last 4 years.

Table 15.1 High School Student Performance on the State ELA and Mathematics Assessment: General Education vs. Special Education

	2007	2008	2009	2010
English Language Arts*				
General Education	83%	94%	94%	95%
Students with Disabilities	34%	33%	29%	20%
Mathematics*				
General Education	86%	94%	94%	96%
Students with Disabilities	34%	31%	30%	20%

* Percentage of students passing

When examining the data, members of the team clearly see the gap in student performance between general education and special education populations.

"Well, I have been here for almost two years," said Mrs. Jones, a high school special education teacher. "And I think that as a school we should be moving toward having a fully inclusionary special education program here at this high school. In the past, the district has had self-contained classes for special education students. But now I think we need to have the special education students be a more interrelated part of the whole high school experience so that they feel part of the high school community."

"I agree," said Mr. Bucket, the school psychologist. "I have been saying for a while that we need to start a newsletter for parents."

"Trying to build relationships with parents at the high school level is very difficult," said Mr. Seiden, a high school English teacher who has been in the school for 15 years. "I have tried to build relationships with parents so they feel that they are valued and that their experiences, as parents of students with disabilities, are the same as students without disabilities in this high school setting."

"At the elementary and middle school level, parents' involvement isn't an issue in the district," said Assistant Principal Bakersfield. "However, when you reach high school, parents think its okay to check out."

"It's probably just as important, if not more so, at the high school," chimed in Mr. Seiden.

"I agree. I think we need to address this issue from multiple perspectives," said Assistant Principal Bakersfield. "I think we need to involve parents more, particularly parents with students with special needs, and I also think we need to revisit discussions surrounding de-tracking and making classes accessible for all special education students."

All members of the action research team shook their heads in agreement. Several took some notes as well.

"We have some students with disabilities, for instance, who want to go to four-year colleges, but they do not have the right math credits, so they have to take the geometry class to be accepted. I have been working to make that a co-taught geometry class. I have been working again with the math department chair—we want to make sure that students get what they need to be able to move on, absolutely to transition," said Ms. Bakersfield.

Again the action research team agreed.

"Okay, I have said what I wanted to," said Ms. Bakersfield. "Now I want to hear from you. What do you think we should do? How can we get all parents involved at the high school level? What can we do to help parents with their child's transition? What has research shown to be the best ways for schools like ours to help address this gap between general education students and students with special needs?"

Ms. Bakersfield took out her notepad and settled in to begin to write down what thoughts or ideas the action research team would generate.

YOUR TURN . . .

Pretend you are a member of the action research team in this case study (or if you are working in a small group, pretend you are the action research team). Develop a list of the additional school data that you would want to examine to gain further knowledge of the high school and the issue that needs to be addressed.

Next, examine the research and literature on addressing the gap between general education students and students with special needs:

- What best practices are supported by the research for school administrators and school leaders in addressing this gap in student performance?
- What does research say about increasing parent involvement in general, as well as the decreased parent involvement commonly found at the high school level?
- What additional data do you need from teachers and related staff to complete the picture?

Next, prepare an overview to present about what you discovered when analyzing past research and literature about the performance gap, models for addressing the performance gap, and promising practices for increasing parent involvement.

After you have presented these findings from the literature, develop an action plan that you would put in place for your school-level action research project. Create another presentation that would outline:

- The program's detail
- The program's timeline
- The program core, interval, and highlight activities
- Any teacher or parent trainings for information sessions that would need to occur.

After you have done that, create an evaluation matrix and develop the instruments and/or data collection points that you would use to monitor the effectiveness of the program your action research team has put in place to address the issue.

CHAPTER 16

Case Study 3: Addressing Behavioral Problems and Low Student Performance

BACKGROUND AND PERSONAL CHARACTERISTICS OF A SCHOOL LEADER

Principal Martin Sanders is confident, professional, and committed to his students, their families, and the overall community of Thompson Academy. He also is an effective leader who understands the importance of leadership theory and knows how to apply it. He sets clear goals and expectations with his staff, as a whole and individually, so no one has to guess later about what he wants.

The outside of Thompson Academy is not inviting. The school is in disrepair. A yellow "Caution" ribbon is strung across its front steps, warning those who pass through of the crumbling cinderblock sidewalk beneath them. In 2006–07, when the case study started, Thompson Academy was on the Schools Under Restricted Review (SURR) list and was in serious danger of being closed by the state if student scores and attendance numbers did not increase. The school serves students in Grades 6 through 8. Enrollment is low, serving approximately 300 students.

Principal Sanders is no stranger to the school. Prior to becoming principal in March 2008, he spent 10 years of his career there as a special education teacher. While a fifth-grade teacher in the school, he "heard the calling" and decided to go back to graduate school and obtain his teacher and district-level administrative certificates. He did his administrative internship at Thompson in 2006–07, before becoming assistant principal in the summer of 2007. In March 2008, the principal left, and Mr. Sanders became acting principal. Because of his unusual experience, Mr. Sanders had a deep understanding of the school, the staff history, and the history of issues that he was up against when he took over the principal position.

LEVEL OF PREPAREDNESS

Overall, Principal Sanders says that graduate course work was valuable and certainly prepared him for the position of administrative leader. "I think overall the literature was relevant and current. I think the program was in itself geared to urban education and helped me specifically address issues that I am dealing with. What I like most about the program is the style of the collaborative work because it helped to demonstrate to me the type of leadership style that I wanted to use with my staff and not a top-down style," he says.

COMMUNITY/LEARNING COMMUNITY. The course work provided him with a perspective for working with his staff and the importance of developing a community in the school. "Giving teachers a more empowered feeling in the school is helpful, especially in urban schools, where stress levels of staff members may be higher than normal. It gives people more ownership in whatever decision or path they take. That overarching theme of the program, I thought, was very powerful. I also thought having us present in large groups, having to present to people, and then forcing us to do that, made me grow from feeling uncomfortable in doing those kinds of things to feeling comfortable. This was a great benefit to us in the end," he said.

DEVELOPMENTAL THEORIES/ADULT DEVELOPMENT. As a reflective practitioner, Mr. Sanders says that one area in which he could have used a little more course work, now that he is in the position of principal, is a course about how to work with adults. One of the biggest challenges of this job is working with adults: parents, teachers, and school staff. He says he would like to know more about counseling and organizational psychology so he could learn to deal better with adults.

As for the talents that Principal Sanders brings to the school, he believes his main talent is a therapy approach to leadership. He also believes he may take this approach because of his special education background. "When I have to have uncomfortable conversations, I think you can always approach people with a certain amount of dignity and disarmament—that is what I bring," he said.

"Another talent that I think I bring is putting forth my expectations of what I think people's goals are and my expectations about them on an ongoing basis, so that there are no surprises when something comes to a head. I am really trying to be proactive in providing core expectations that I have for people right from the beginning."

INSTRUCTIONAL LEADERSHIP. Although Principal Sanders says that he misses the classroom from time to time, he also says that he recognizes that when he made the switch from assistant principal to acting principal, and then the jump to head principal, he really tried to make the switch to focus on instruction. "I am able to delegate and not have my hand in everything," he says.

SUPERVISION. One of the challenges Mr. Sanders faced was becoming principal in the middle of the school year. He says that things were already "set in motion" when he assumed the position. For example, the former principal had already determined which new teachers would stay on; however, based on his own observations of the teachers, Principal Sanders said he had his own idea as to which new teachers showed promise and demonstrated effective instructional practices in the classrooms.

LEADERSHIP THEORIES/FOSTERING RELATIONSHIPS. In addition, Principal Sanders had spent much of the year as acting principal, working with faculty to create a positive climate and to help teachers focus instruction toward student strengths and not their weaknesses.

LEADERSHIP THEORIES. While working with faculty over the course of the last year, Mr. Sanders has tried to implement his vision, but he always recognized the high rate of staff turnover and that he had to be sympathetic without bringing about too many new initiatives. In his first year as school principal, Mr. Sanders saw his role as an instructional leader trying to support the curriculum that was already in place and to be very clear with his expectations for faculty.

STEP 1: ESTABLISHING AN ACTION RESEARCH TEAM

Understanding that it would be impossible for him to take on the action research process by himself, Principal Sanders forms a mixed-panel action research team. Because of past events and poor relationships in the school between administration and staff (and because he was a former teacher in the school), Principal Sanders decides to use the advisory role approach to form the school's action research team. He selects three grade-level teachers, the school psychologist, the school social worker, and an outspoken parent. At a meeting, Principal Sanders announces who will make up the action research team. Afterward, several members of the team approach him and inform him that they are surprised and taken aback with his choice of the parent representative for the committee. They tell Principal Sanders that they are not opposed to having a parent voice on the team, that in fact they think it is a good thing; however, they are opposed to having this particular parent and do not want to serve on the committee if he does not select another parent. Principal Sanders stands firm on his decision and replaces the three grade-level teachers.

STEP 2: ANALYZING THE SCHOOL

One of the first responsibilities of the school-level action research team is to come together, examine the school data, and have a rich discussion. All members of the team find the school's archival data to be dismal. In 2007–08, student performance on the state's ELA assessment was low: 45% of sixth-graders passed, 39% of seventh-graders, and only 14% of eighth-graders. On the state's mathematics assessment, 60% of sixth-graders passed, 38% of seventh-graders, and 22% of eighth-graders. Forty-six percent (46%) of students passed the state's Science 8

Table 16.1 Principal Sanders' Impact on Thompson Academy and ELA and Math Assessment Scores

	2005–06	2006–07**	2007–08	2008–09
ELA*				
Grade 6	25%	50%	45%	45%
Grade 7	25%	24%	39%	34%
Grade 8	15%	15%	14%	23%
Math*				
Grade 6				
Grade 7				
Grade 8				

* % students passing
** Time period prior to Mr. Sanders becoming school principal

assessments. All of the grades are well below the average when compared to schools with similar characteristics.

In addition, issues surrounding student behavior have increased, including student absenteeism and unexcused absences. Office referrals have increased 67% over the course of the last 4 years (2005–06 to 2008–09). Unexcused absences also have increased 57%. In further examination of these data, the action research team discovers that 80% of the office referrals are attributed to approximately 20 individuals from across sixth through eighth grades. Of the unexcused absences, 79% also are attributed to these same 20 or so students.

"It is interesting that when you examine the unexcused absences and office referrals by individual students, you see that the problem isn't across the school but really with a handful of students," said Mr. Jackson, the school psychologist.

"And when you look at who these students are, it really isn't a surprise," said Miss Turner, the school social worker. "I know these students and I am sure that many of you do, too."

"We really need a program that addresses all behaviors in a school but also focuses on targeting the students who are the most challenging," said one of the grade-level teachers.

"We've got to get parents involved, too," said Mrs. Johnston, the parent whom Principal Sanders had purposefully selected for the team. "You don't know what these kids' home life is like. It's no wonder they don't come to school and don't behave when they get there. We've got to get the families on board."

The other team members are surprised at Mrs. Johnston's calm and rational behavior. They had only known her from PTA meetings where she would often shout over school officials, argue with other parents, and present information that was not factual or accurate. Here, as a member of the action research team, Mrs. Johnson had a new perspective and had become a valuable asset to the team, bringing a fresh and different perspective to the table.

"We need some kind of program that we can implement at the school that targets the behavioral issues and also rewards students for following the rules and making smart choices," said Mr. Jackson.

"And we need to get parents involved," chimed in Mrs. Johnson.

The other members of the team smiled. They all agreed.

After further discussion, the action research team agreed that the school would be best served if some sort of rewards-based behavioral program could be implemented schoolwide and that would address decreasing office referrals and absenteeism and would focus on a range of strategies for the students who proved to be the most challenging through a tier-system approach. The action research team also wanted to develop a program that simultaneously would increase parent involvement in the school.

As the action research team progressed with its work and began to review the literature, Mrs. Johnston shared with the group how appreciative she was to have the opportunity to work on the team with them. She told the team that she was always suspicious of school officials, the school board, the principal, and the teachers at the school. She told them that she thought they were always having secret meetings before the PTA or school board meetings where they really decided on what was going to happen. She said that she never knew so much work or dedication went into the work everyone did in trying to come up with ways to address issues in the school and make it a better and more productive place for learning. Mrs. Johnston also said that she had been telling all the parents about the hard work the action research team was doing, all the long hours and data that they were collecting and analyzing, and how important it was for parents to come to the next meeting where the action research team would present the plan to the parents, teachers, and principal.

YOUR TURN . . .

Pretend you are a member of the action research team (or if you are working in a small group pretend you are the action research team). Develop a list of the additional school data that you would want to examine to gain further knowledge of the issues surrounding student performance, student behavior, and parent involvement.

Next, examine the research and literature on addressing a rewards-based behavioral program or models for middle schools and increased parent involvement at the middle school.

- What additional data do you need from teachers and related staff to complete the picture?

Next, prepare an overview to present what you discovered when analyzing past research and literature about the behavioral programs for middle school students.

After you have presented these findings from the literature, develop an action plan that you would put in place for your school-level action research project. Create another presentation that would outline the following:

- The program's detail
- The program's timeline
- The program core, interval, and highlight activities
- Any teacher or parent trainings for information sessions that would need to occur

After you have done that, create an evaluation matrix and develop the instruments and/or data collection points that you would use to monitor the effectiveness of the program your action research team has put in place to address the issue. For further assistance on evaluation matrices refer back to Chapter 6. Then answer the following questions:

- What do you think about Principal Sanders's leadership style?
- How would you describe it?
- How do you see his leadership style playing into his action research team design?
- What do you think are the benefits and/or limitations of his decision to select the formerly vocal parent?

CHAPTER 17

Case Study 4: Improving Low ELA Scores at the Elementary Level

SCHOOL LEADER

Principal Janet Miles is a confident, self-motivated, progressive administrator with strong connections to the classroom, teaching, and providing optimum instruction for all students in her school. One of Principal Miles's strong suits is that she has an extensive background in curriculum and instruction at the elementary levels. Becoming a principal at Gilford Academy is Mrs. Miles's first position as a school administrator; however, prior to becoming the principal, she was a teacher for 7 years at another elementary school in the same district. In her teaching position, Mrs. Miles taught kindergarten, third grade, and fourth grade. Principal Miles believes that her background as a teacher provides her with a strong connection to the curriculum as a school principal. She also believes that her strong background gives her immediate respect and buy-in from her teaching staff that she does not think she would get otherwise. She says, "Knowing the curriculum inside and out and knowing how it should look and function in a classroom [and being able to engage with her teachers in a deep conversation about it] gives her a tremendous amount of credibility." She says that many times principals may not have that in-depth knowledge about a curriculum, and teachers quickly pick up on that.

SCHOOL DISTRICT

The Gilford Academy is part of a city school district and serves a community comprised of mostly African American students. With an enrollment of about 354 students, the school is made up of approximately 86% Black, 8% Hispanic, and 4% White students. Of the student body, 76% is eligible for free or reduced-price lunch. Gilford Academy has 41 teachers with 3% holding a master's degree or higher. According to the financial information provided by the State Report Card 2006–07, Gilford Academy, on average, spends a total of $17,276 per pupil; compared to the rest of the state's public schools, this is higher by about $10,000.

Overall, the students at Gilford Academy are meeting the required standards presented to them. All of the students are in good standing in all subject areas, and the school has received Title I Part A Funding.

LEVEL OF PREPAREDNESS

Reflecting on her school administrator course work, Principal Miles sees a strong connection between the courses and her position as a school principal in an urban school setting. "I definitely see the relevance of my graduate course work in educational leadership to the position," she says. "When I think about the first part of the course work when we started to think about what leadership is and understanding oneself as a leader, I think that was critical. That I could be the type of leader that I wanted to be, that there wasn't just one particular style of leader out there—learning who you are as a person and working as a leader with the personality that you have. That was really the focal point of those first courses. Those courses really made you dig deep into who you are, and took you through the leadership styles—and I think that that was foundational."

CURRICULUM AUDITING AND EVALUATION. Principal Miles also found a strong connection to her role as a principal as well as to the activities that she conducts as a curriculum leader. "My graduate course on curriculum was critical because it is important to know what your teachers need and to figure out ways, as an administrator, to effectively support them in the classroom by knowing the curriculum as well as or better [in some cases] than the teachers. That is something that I have been very focused on here. My teachers are often surprised at how in depth I know the curriculum, and that brings a lot of credibility to me as a first-year administrator. It also helps me, because I know how they are teaching and I can suggest ways to help them 'lift' their teaching. They can see I am trying to help them."

COMMUNITY/LEARNING COMMUNITY. "Engaging communities is huge, because it really does focus on issues surrounding and engaging urban schools, and how as a leader you can create a positive climate in which children can be successful, which is often the opposite of the picture that is painted of urban schools. That course was really important," she says. Principal Miles uses what she learned about building community every day in her position, making her a more effective leader.

Principal Miles says that her courses on supervision play a major role as a school administrator. "The supervision courses really helped us see all the work that goes into teacher evaluation—talking about the snapshot picture that you may see when you are in the classroom versus understanding what is going on in that classroom all the time from a much more holistic perspective. I have really tried to work on that understanding, as difficult as it can be, when you have a stack of work to do," she says.

SCHOOL COMMUNITY/LEARNING COMMUNITY. "The biggest things I took away from my graduate course work in educational leadership are that it was okay to be supportive of my teachers. I learned through my course work that 'Leadership is stewardship' and that you have to support your teachers to make it possible for them to do the work that you want them to do. That is what I have tried to do here, in addition to trying to push them to be stronger." She continues, "The instructional piece is the part that I really enjoy the most, and I know that it is the part of the administrator role that keeps me connected to the classroom."

She says that her teachers see the amount of time, work, and energy she puts into providing them with feedback from her observations, which in part she is able to do because she has such a strong instructional background. She thinks about what they are doing when she conducts an evaluation and carefully considers what feedback would help the teacher grow. Principal Miles thinks that this is a key piece—supporting teachers any way that she can—if she wants her staff to grow as professionals and become more effective in their work. In her first year, Principal Miles focused on making changes in the school and addressing certain issues, such as attendance and discipline, critical matters that were not defined operationally as well as they should be. In addition, she also worked on setting up times that teachers could meet and work with her. "Now that those things are in place, now that I look at our school improvement plan, the one thing that jumps out at me, and is very much in need of attention, is our parent piece. It's weak, in the sense that it is not an organized parent piece; parents can't regularly meet and have discussions. It's the same core of parents, so the one thing I want to have us work on as a goal for next year is to work on our PTA piece. I would like to have us begin to grow our K–2 level, to have parents grow and be able to give us constant feedback," she says.

In addition, Principal Miles is focused on setting curriculum expectations for every grade level. She has been working with teachers to sit down with the grade levels above and below them and to have discussions about what aspects students do well and what aspects they still need to work on. "I think it was a very eye-opening experience for the teachers," she says. "Many of the teachers thought certain curricula were taught at certain grade levels, when in fact they hadn't been. This has become a very important conversation that we have now documented in our mission to focus on good teaching," she said.

STEP 1: ESTABLISHING THE ACTION RESEARCH TEAM

The first step that Principal Miles takes is to assemble an action research team. Recognizing that the school's issue pertaining to literacy is to improve student performance on the state's ELA assessment, she selects two teachers from each of the three grades. She also selects the school psychologist to serve on the team, since she knows the school psychologist has the in-depth knowledge regarding assessment and standardized measures such as norm-grouped, criterion, and self-referent. In addition, she includes two of the school's literacy coaches.

STEP 2: ANALYZING SCHOOL DATA

On their first meeting, the action research team began to examine the systems/accountability data for their school. In addition to examining the most recent data available to them, they also went back and examined the past several years to establish more of a baseline.

Several of the teachers made comments about the improvements the school had made on the state's ELA assessments over the course of the last few years.

"We really have made some nice gains on the ELA," said Mr. Valder, a third-grade teacher who has been at the school for 7 years. "It's nice to see all the hard work we did in professional development and implementing the new curriculum finally paying off."

"The new curriculum has been a hard sell to teachers," said Mrs. Stevenson, one of the school's literacy coaches. "But you're right. Now that teachers have all been trained in the new literacy program, they are really starting to see it work in their classrooms, and that makes a big difference, too."

Table 17.1 Students' Performance on State's Criterion-Based ELA Assessment

ELA (% Students at Levels 3 & 4)	2004–2005	2005–2006	2006–2007	2008–09
Grade 3	69%	70%	81%	85%
Grade 4	69%	78%	82%	82%
Grade 5	65%	76%	80%	81%

"Making real change is hard," said Mrs. Bedford, a fourth-grade teacher who was new to the school.

"One of the things that I can't figure out," said Principal Miles, "is yes, if you look at our student performance on the state's ELA assessment, we are showing improvements each year. However, if you look at other measures that we give our students we aren't progressing as rapidly."

The room went silent. Everyone looked at Principal Miles.

"What do you mean?" said one of the other teachers. "Our scores are increasing aren't they?"

"Yes," replied Principal Miles, "our school's scores are improving."

"So what is the problem?" asked Mr. Bedford.

"The problem is that when you do a comparison analysis, and compare our school scores to another standardized measure, we haven't made the same gains," explained Principal Miles.

"So we haven't made the improvements?" questioned Mr. Bedford.

"Well, we have," said Principal Miles. "But remember the state test is criterion-based measures, and the reading assessment we give to our students throughout the year is a norm-grouped assessment."

Principal Miles went on to explain to her staff that criterion-based measures have a cut score and that the cut score is arbitrarily set by the state. A student's performance on a criterion-based measure is interpreted through some criteria. In the case of the state test, these criteria are the state learning standards. Students' raw scores are converted to scaled scores, and those scales reflect the level of student performance. On the state assessments, if students are working on Levels 1 and 2, they are not meeting benchmarks, whereas students receiving Levels 3 and 4 scores indicate students who are making progress. Student performance on a norm-grouped assessment is interpreted through the norms groups or populations from whom the test is created. On norm-grouped assessments, students' raw scores are interpreted through the normal distribution in relation to standard deviations. A student increasing a standard deviation would most

Table 17.2 Student Performance on Normed-Group Reading and Comprehension Assessment

ELA (% Students at Levels 3 & 4)	2005–2006	2006–2007	2007–2008
Grade 3	56%	53%	40%
Grade 4	58%	55%	37%
Grade 5	55%	55%	54%

likely be a valid indicator of growth or success, compared to a student moving from a high Level 2 to a low Level 3 on a criterion-based assessment.

"I am not saying that the state test isn't accurate," explained Principal Miles. "What I am saying is that as a school we are trying our hardest to improve student performance in the school, and we cannot use the state's criterion-based measure as our only guiding light."

Principal Miles went on to explain that they needed to create a multifaceted plan to better monitor their school's progress in regard to literacy and student performance in ELA. If they truly wanted to track the successes (and failures) of their efforts, they were going to need to come up with a more sophisticated system.

YOUR TURN . . .

Either individually or in your action research team, develop a better method for monitoring the impact of the school's new literacy initiative. Develop a logic model and an evaluation matrix. Make sure that you have data from all three sources (i.e., systems/accountability, school/program, and classroom). In addition, make sure that you also have included assessments that are criterion, norm-grouped, and self-referent, if possible. Then present your matrix and logic model to the class.

REFERENCES

Abernathy, S. F. (2007). *No Child Left Behind and the public schools.* Ann Arbor: University of Michigan Press.

Beecher, M., & Sweeny, S. M. (2008). Closing the achievement gap with curriculum enrichment and differentiation: One school's story. *Journal of Advanced Academics, 19*(3), 502–530.

Bennett, C. K. (1994, Winter). Promoting teacher reflection through action research: What do teachers think? *Journal of Staff Development 15*(1), 34–38.

Bernhardt, V. L. (1999, June). Invited Monograph No. 5. Oroville, CA: California Association for Supervision and Curriculum Development (CASCD).

Bernhardt, V. L. (2000). Intersections: new routes open when one type of data crosses another. *Journal of Staff Development, 1*(21), 33–36.

Bernhardt, V. L. (2003). No schools left behind. *Educational leadership, 60*(5), 26–30.

Bernhardt, V. L. (2004, November/December). Continuous improvement: It takes more than test scores. *ACSA Leadership,* 16–19.

Bernhardt, V. L. (2005). Data tools for school improvement. *Educational Leadership, 62*(5), 66–69.

Bernhardt, V. L. (2009). Data use: Data-driven decision making takes a big-picture view of the needs of teachers and students. *Journal of Staff Development, 1*(30), 24–27.

Berry, B., Trantham, P., & Wade, C. (2008). Using data, changing teaching. *Educational Leadership,* 80–84.

Calhoun, E. F. (1994). *How to use action research in the self-renewing school.* Alexandria, VA: Association for Supervision and Curriculum Development.

Calhoun, E. F. (2002). Action research for school. *Educational Leadership,* 18–24.

Campbell, D. T., & Stanley, J. (1963). *Experimental and quasi-experimental design for research.* Chicago: Rand McNally.

Chan-Remka, J. (2007). The perceptions of teachers and administrators in relation to the implementation of professional learning communities. *Dissertation Abstracts International Section A: Humanities and Social Sciences, 68*(6-A), 2411.

Corey, S. M. (1953). *Action research to improve school practices.* New York: Teachers College Press.

Danielson, C. (2001). New trends in teacher evaluation. *Educational Leadership, 58*(5), 12–15.

Darling-Hammond, L. (2010). *The flat world and education: How America's commitment to equity will determine our future.* New York: Teachers College Press.

Del Favero, F. (2009). Using data to affect school change: A critical leadership skill serving as the keystone of the school improvement process. *The Connexions Project.* Retrieved September 6, 2011, from http://cnx.org/content/m32036/1.1

Doran, H. C. (2003). Adding value to accountability. *Educational Leadership, 61*(3), 55–59.

Ellingsen, J. (2007, September). Data unwrapped. *Leadership, 59*(6), 22–23.

Ferguson, C. K. (2008). A national study to determine data usage of principals for school improvement. *Dissertation Abstracts International Section A: Humanities and Social Sciences, 68*(11-A), 45–58.

Fleischman, S. (2006, March). Moving to evidence-based professional practice. *Educational Leadership, 63*(6), 87–89.

Frechtling, J. A. (2007). *Logic modeling in program evaluation.* San Francisco: Jossey-Bass Wiley.

Fullan, M. (2004). *Leadership and sustainability: System thinkers in action.* Thousand Oaks, CA: Corwin Press.

Fusarelli, L. D. (2008, January). Flying (partially) blind: School leaders' use of research in decision making. *Phi Delta Kappan,* 365–368.

Glanz, J. (1999). A primer on action research for the school administrator. *The Clearing House, 72*(5), 301–304.

Glickman, C. D., Gordon, S. P., & Ross-Gordon, J. M. (2007). *SuperVision and instructional leadership: A developmental approach.* New York: Pearson.

Gold, S. (2005). Driven by data: How three districts are successfully using data, rather than gut feelings, to align staff development with school needs. *Technology & Learning, 25*(11), 6–9.

Goldring, E., & Berends, M. (2009). *Leading with data: Pathways to improve your school.* Thousand Oaks, CA: Corwin Press.

Green, R. L. (2010). *The four dimensions of principal leadership: A framework for leading 21st century schools.* Boston: Allyn & Bacon.

Guskey, T. (2000). *Evaluating professional development.* Thousand Oaks, CA: Corwin Press.

Guskey, T. R. (2002). Professional development and teacher change. *Teachers and Teaching: Theory and practice, 8*(3/4), 381–391.

Hahs-Vaughn, D. L., & Yanowitz, K. L. (2009). Who is conducting teacher research? *The Journal of Educational Research, 102*(6), 415–424.

Heifitz, R. (1998). *Leadership without easy answers.* Cambridge, MA: Harvard University Press.

Hess, F. M. (2008). The new stupid. *Educational Leadership, 66*(4), 12–17.

Hurley, S. (2010, January 31). *Trends in education: How they come and go.* Retrieved September 2, 2011, from www.edutopia.org/educational-trends-bandwagons

Johnston, D. A., & Lawrence, J. T. (2004). Using data to inform instruction. *Leadership, 34*(2), 28–29, 35.

Likert, R. (1932). A technique for the measurement of attitudes. *Archives of Psychology 140,* 1–55.

Kelsay, K. L. (1991, Spring). When experience is the best teacher: The teacher as researcher. *Action in Teacher Education, 13*(1), 14–21.

Killion, J. (2008). *Assessing impact: Evaluating staff development.* Thousand Oaks, CA: Corwin Press and NSCD.

Kirkpatrick, D. L. (1998). *Another look at evaluating training programs.* Alexandria, VA: American Society for Training & Development.

Ladd, G. T. (1916, June 18). Our many educational fads and fancies. *New York Times.* SM 13.

Lodico, M. G., Spaulding, D. T., & Voegtle, K. H. (2010). *Methods in Educational Research: From Theory to Practice.* San Francisco: Jossey-Bass Wiley.

Marzano, R. J. (2003). *What works in schools: Translating research into action.* Alexandria, VA: Association for Supervision and Curriculum Development.

Marzano, R. J., Pickering, D. J., & Pollock, J. E. (2001). *Classroom instruction that works: Research-based strategies for increasing student achievement.* Alexandria, VA: Association for Supervision and Curriculum Development.

Marzano, R. J., Walters, T., & McNulty, B. A. (2005). *School leadership that works: From research to results.* Aurora, CO: Mid-continent Research for Education and Learning.

Mathison, S. (2004). *Encyclopedia of evaluation.* Thousand Oaks, CA: Sage.

McGuinn, P. J. (2006). *No Child Left Behind and the transformation of federal education policy, 1965–2005.* Lawrence: University Press of Kansas.

McLeod, S. (2005). Technology tools for data-driven teachers. University Council for Education Administration (UCEA) Center for the Advanced Study of Technology Leadership in Education (CASTLE). Retrieved October 6, 2011, from academic.research.microsoft.com/Paper/6771575.

Miller, D. M., & Pine, G. J. (1990, Summer). Advancing professional inquiry for educational improvement through action research. *Journal of Staff Development, 11*(3), 56–61.

Mills, G. E. (2010). *Action research: A guide for the teacher researcher.* Upper Saddle River, NJ: Prentice Hall.

National Commission on Excellence in Education (1983). *A nation at risk: The imperative for educational reform.* Washington, DC: Author. Retrieved September 2, 2011, from www2.ed.gov/pubs/NatAtRisk/title.html

Phillips, J. J. (1997). The ROI process model. In *Handbook of training evaluation* (3rd ed., pp. 66–78). Waltham, MA: Butterworth-Heinemann.

Ravitch, D. (2000). *Left back: A century of failed school reforms.* New York: Simon & Schuster.

Reeves, D. B. (2008). Looking deeper into data. *Educational Leadership, 66*(4), 89–90.

Reilly, M. A. (2007). Choice of action: using data to make instructional decisions in kindergarten. *The Reading Teacher, 60*(8), 770–776.

Sagor, R. How to conduct collaborative action research. Alexandria, VA: Association for Supervision and Curriculum Development.

Schmoker, M. (2010). When pedagogic fads trump priorities. *Education Week, 30*(5), 22–23.

Seaton, M., Emmett, R. E., Welsh, K., & Petrossian, A. (2008). Teaming up for teaching and learning. *Leadership, 37*(3), 26–29.

Stiggins, M., & Duke, D. (2008, December). Effective instructional leadership requires assessment leadership. *Phi Delta Kappan*, 285–291.

Streifer, P. A., & Schumann, J. A. (2005). Using data mining to identify actionable information: Breaking new ground in data-driven decision making. *Journal of Education for Students Placed at Risk, 10*(3), 281–293.

Strickland, D. S. (1989, December). The teacher as researcher: Toward the extended professional. *Language Arts, 65*(8), 754–764.

Taylor, F.W. (1967). *Principles of scientific management.* New York: Norton.

Technology Alliance. (2005). Publication and policy: Data-driven decision-making in K-12 schools. Retrieved September 6, 2011, from www.technology-alliance.com/pubspols/dddm/dddm.html

Tyack, D., & Cuban, L. (1995). *Tinkering toward utopia: A century of public school reform.* Cambridge, MA: Harvard University Press.

Waters, T., & Cameron, G. (2007). *The balanced leadership framework: Connecting vision with action.* Denver, CO: Mid-continent Research for Education and Learning.

Wayman, J. C. (2005). Involving teachers in data-driven decision making: Using computer data systems to support teacher inquiry and reflection. *Journal of Education for Students Placed at Risk, 10*(3), 295–308.

Weiss, C. (1997). *Evaluation.* Upper Saddle River, NJ: Prentice Hall.

Whitaker, T. (2003). *What great principals do differently: Fifteen things that matter most.* Larchmont, NY: Eye on Education.

Wolf, D. P., LeMahieu, P. G., & Eresh, J. (1992). Good measure: Assessment as a tool for educational reform. *Educational Leadership, 49*(8) 8–13.

INDEX

A

Abernathy, S., 4
Abstracts, 50
Accountability data, 40
    institutional/policy, 111–112
Action research. *See* Classroom action research; School action research; System/district-wide action research
Action research teams
    See also Data analysis
    defined, 31
    role of, 30, 31–33
    types of, 33–35
Activities, 96–97, 121
Administrators, research used by, 11–14
Advisory/managerial design, 34
AIMSweb, 114
American Psychological Association (APA) style, 14
Analysis
    See also Data analysis
    baseline, 41
    concurrent validity, 44
    disaggregation, 41–43
    longitudinal/cohort, 43
    trend, 43
Applied research, 14–15
Archival data, 64
ARLIN Test of Formal Reasoning, 117
Assessments
    See also Standardized measures
    classroom-level, 112
    criterion-referenced, 113–114
    institutional/policy accountability, 111–112
    levels of, 110–112
    needs, 39–41
    norm-referenced, 113
    program-level, 112
    reliability of, 114–115
    role of, 6
    self-referenced, 114
    validity of, 115
Autonomy design, 34–35

B

Bandwagon principle, 7
Baseline, 41
Behavioral problems, case study
    action research team formation, 140
    data analysis, 140–141
    preparedness levels, 139–140
    school leader characteristics, 138
Bernhardt, V. L., 39
Bivariate studies, 62

Body of the survey, 82
Bootstrap data, 8
Bounded system, 74
Bush, G. H. W., 3

C

California Achievement Test (CAT), 113
Cameron, G., 5
Case studies, 74
Causal-comparative research, 57–58
Causality, 61–62
Cause-and-effect research, 53–54
Checklists, 72, 83–84, 86
Clinton, B., 3
Classroom action research
    assessment of findings, 25–26
    defined, 16, 19
    identification of problems/needs, 22
    instructional methods, deciding on, 22–23
    instructional methods, evaluation of, 23–25
    natural, 20–21
    steps in, 21
    teacher provided instruction, 22
Classroom-level assessments, 112
Cluster sampling, 66–67
Concurrent validity, 44, 115
Construct validity, 115
Content validity, 115
Core activities, 96
Corey, S. M., 16
Correlational coefficient, 62
Correlational matrix, 63
Correlational research
    applications, 64
    causality and, 61–62
    purpose of, 61
    reliability and validity measures, 64
    sample size, 65
    shotgun approach, 65
    statistical significance, 63
    types of, 62–63
Criterion-referenced assessments, 113–114
Criterion-related validity, 115
Criterion variable, 63
Cuban, L., 3
Cut score, 113–114

D

Darling-Hammond, L., 2
Data
    accountability, 40

Data (*Continued*)
  archival, 64
  baseline, 41
  school archival, 39–41
  student performance, 40–41
Data analysis
  See also Assessments
  example of, 37–38
  how to conduct, 38–39
  needs assessment, 39–41
  techniques, 41–44
Data-based decision making, 39
Databases, 48
Demographics, 81–82
Directions, 81
Disaggregation analysis, 41–43
Duke, D., 16, 39, 40, 41, 110, 111, 112, 114, 116

E

Education
  changing role of, 1–4
  purpose of, 5
  trends, problems with, 7–8
Educational Resources Information Center (ERIC), 48
Elementary and Secondary Education Act (ESEA) (1965), 2, 3
Empirical research, 49
Equivalent-form reliability, 114–115
Ethnographic research, 74–75
Experimental research, 54–57
Ex post facto research, 58

F

Feedback
  collecting, 78, 80
  formative, 103
Feedback loops
  outcomes, end, 124–125
  outcomes, intermediate, 122–123
  purpose of, 122
  summative, 126
Fidelity
  checklist and observational protocol, 104–106
  defined, 103–104
  formative feedback, 103
  of professional development, 107–108
Fleishman, S., 12–14
Focus group, 24
Frechtling, J. A., 95, 96, 97
Fullan, M., 98
Fusarelli, L. S., 11, 12–14

G

Gates-MacGinitie assessment, 113
Glickman, C. D., 8
Goals 2000, 3, 4
Gordon, S. P., 8
Green, R. L., 106
Guskey, T., 107

H

Hand-out, mail-back, 88, 89–90
Hand-out and collect in drop box, 88, 90
Hand-out and collect on site, 88, 90
Heifitz, R., 5
Hess, F. M., 6
Homogenous, 67
Hurley, S., 7
Hypothesis, 50

I

Improving America's Schools Act (1994), 3–4
Industrial Age, education during, 2
Inputs, 95–96
Institutional/policy accountability, 111–112
Internal consistency, 114
Inter-observer reliability, 104
Interview protocol, 72
Iowa Test of Basic Skills (ITBS), 113
Item validity, 115

J

Johnson, L., 2

K

Killion, J., 107
Kirkpatrick, D. L., 107

L

Ladd, G. T., 7
Leadership Without Easy Answers (Heifitz), 5
Levels of Impact model
  Level 1: classroom action research, 16, 19–26
  Level 2: school action research, 16, 28–36
  Level 3: system/district-wide action research, 17
Likert, L., 83
Likert scales, 83
Literature
  See also Research
  abstracts, 50
  matrix, 52–53
  organizing and extracting information, 49–52
  use of term, 49
Logic models
  See also Feedback loops
  activities, 96–97, 121
  applications, 99–100
  defined, 94
  example of, 95

inputs, 95–96
modifying, 120–126
outcomes, 97–98, 122–125
outputs, 97, 121–122
reasons for using, 94
standardized measures and, 115–117
theory of change, 99
Longitudinal/cohort analysis, 43

M

Mail-out, mail-back, 87–89
Mail to site with point person to administer, 88, 90–91
Matching, 58
Mathison, S., 96
Member checks, 73
Metropolitan Achievement Test (MAT), 113
Mid-Continent research for Education and Learning (McREL), 5
Mixed methods, 26
Mixed-panel teams, 33
Multiple regression, 63

N

Narrative inquiry, 74
National Assessment for Educational Progress (NAEP), 114
National Commission on Excellence in Education, 2
National Standards for Arts Education, 3
Nation at Risk, A, 2–3
Needs assessment, 39–41
"New Stupid, The" (Hess), 6
No Child Left Behind (NCLB) Act, 4
No Child Left Behind and the Public Schools (Abernathy), 4
Nonrandomized sample, 67
Norm group, 113
Norm-referenced assessments, 113

O

Observational protocols, 72, 104–106
Observer bias, 73
Observer effect, 73
Open-ended items, 84
"Our Many Educational Fads and Fancies" (Ladd), 7
Outcomes, 97–98
    end, 124–125
    intermediate, 122–123
Outputs, 97, 121–122

P

Participatory design, 34
Peer-reviewed journals, 14
Performance gaps, case study
    action research team formation, 135

data analysis, 135–136
preparedness levels, 134–135
school leader characteristics, 133–134
Phenomenological research, 75
Phillips, J. J., 107
Piaget, J., 117
Population, 66
Prediction studies, 63
Predictor variable, 63
Professional development, evaluating, 106–108
Program development, 93–94
    See also Logic models
Program implementation. *See* Fidelity
Program-level assessments, 112
Protocols, 23, 25
    observational, 72, 104–106
PsycARTICLES, 48
PsycINFO, 48
p-value, 63

Q

Qualitative research
    access to subjects and settings, 72–73
    applications, 75
    compared with other methods, 71–72
    examples of, 74
    techniques, 72
    types of, 74–75
Quasi- experimental research, 57

R

Randomization, 54
Random sampling, 66–67
Ravitch, D., 7
Reagan, R., 2
Reeves, D. B., 6
Reliability
    equivalent-form, 114–115
    internal consistency, 114
    inter-observer, 104
    measures, 64, 114–115
    split-half, 114
    test-retest, 114
    versus validity, 115
Research
    See also Literature
    abstracts, 50
    action, 15–16
    administrators' use of, 11–14
    applied, 14–15
    causal-comparative, 57–58
    cause-and-effect, 53–54
    components, 49
    correlational, 61–65, 69

Research (*Continued*)
  databases, 48
  empirical, 49
  ethnographic, 74–75
  examining past, 47–48
  experimental, 54–57
  ex post facto, 58
  hypothesis, 50
  Levels of Impact model, 16–17
  phenomenological, 75
  qualitative, 71–76
  survey, 65–69
  vendor, 15
Response rates, 67–68
Ross-Gordon, J. M., 8

S

Sample bias, 68
Sample of convenience, 67
Sample size, 65, 67
Sampling
  cluster, 66–67
  random, 66–67
  validity, 115
Scales, 82
Schmoker, M., 7
School action research
  defined, 16
  identifying issues, 30
  program assessment, 30
  program development, 30
  program implementation, 30
  program modifications, 31
  steps in, 29
  teams, role of, 30, 31–33
  teams, type of, 33–35
School archival data, 39–41
School leaders/leadership
  factors affecting the changing role of, 1–4
  importance of, 4–6
Self-referenced assessments, 114
Semantic differential scales, 83
Shotgun approach, 65
Single stakeholder-based teams, 33
Split-half reliability, 114
Standardized measures
  criterion-referenced, 113–114
  defined, 113
  logic models and, 115–117
  norm-referenced, 113
  reliability of, 114–115
  self-referenced, 114
  types of, 112–113
  validity of, 115

Standards-based movement, 3, 4
Stanford Achievement Test, 113
Statistical significance, 63
Stiggins, M., 16, 39, 40, 41, 110, 111, 112, 114, 116
Stratified random sampling, 66–67
Student performance and ELA scores, case study
  action research team formation, 145
  data analysis, 145–147
  preparedness levels, 144–145
  school district, description of, 143–144
  school leader characteristics, 143
Student performance data, 40–41
Summative feedback loops, 126
Survey research
  adapting instruments from, 69
  applications, 65
  design and development, 69
  population, 66
  random sampling, 66–67
  response rates, 67–68
  role of, 65
  sample bias, 68
  sample size, 67
Surveys
  administering, 87–91
  components of, 81–84
  effects of poorly constructed, 81
  example of, 79
  feedback from, 78, 80
  hand-out, mail-back, 88, 89–90
  hand-out and collect in drop box, 88, 90
  hand-out and collect on site, 88, 90
  mail-out, mail-back, 87–89
  mail to site with point person to administer, 88, 90–91
  role of, 80–81
  writing tips, 85–87
System/district-wide action research, 17

T

Teacher turnover, case study
  action research team formation, 129–130
  data analysis, 130–131
  data collection from staff, 132
  literature review, 132
  school leader characteristics, 128–129
Teams. *See* Action research teams
TerraNova, 113
Test-retest reliability, 114
Tests of Academic Proficiency (TAP), 113
Theory of change, 99
Trend analysis, 43
Tyack, D., 3

V

Validity
  concurrent, 44, 115
  construct, 115
  content, 115
  criterion-related, 115
  item, 115
  measures, 64, 115
  purpose of, 115
  sampling, 115
  versus reliability, 115
Vendor research, 15

W

Waters, T., 5
"When Pedagogic Fads Trump Priorities" (Schmoker), 7